Russell Westbrook: The Inspiring Story of One of Basketball's Premier Point Guards

An Unauthorized Biography

D1416142

By: Clayton Geoffreys

Table of Contents

Foreword

Whenever someone talks about the Oklahoma City Thunder, two players immediately come to mind: Kevin Durant and Russell Westbrook. Though Durant is generally known as the leader of the Oklahoma City Thunder, Russell Westbrook has proven himself to be just as important of a cornerstone piece for the basketball franchise. Sorely missed in the 2013 NBA Playoffs due to an injury of game two in the first round of the playoffs, Russell Westbrook poses himself as a deadly scoring threat on the basketball court. Russell's rise to stardom is no mistake—his story truly begins when he was still in high school, struggling to make his high school varsity team until his junior year. His journey would continue into college as he spent much of his freshman year on the bench before getting his opportunity to shine in his sophomore year, ultimately having a successful enough season to be selected with the fourth overall pick of the 2008 NBA Draft. Thank you for downloading *Russell Westbrook: The Inspiring Story of One of Basketball's Premier Point Guards*. In this unauthorized biography, we will learn Russell's incredible life story and impact on the game of basketball. Hope you enjoy and if you do, please do not forget to leave a review! Also, check out my website at claytongeoffreys.com to join my exclusive list where I let you know about my latest books and give you goodies!

Cheers,

Clayton Geoffreys

Visit me at www.claytongeoffreys.com

Introduction

Russell Westbrook cannot play for a contending team. He is selfish. He makes bad decisions on the court. He takes the ball away from great offensive players like Kevin Durant and James Harden. He is just another athletic "me-first" point guard, and the Thunders would be better off without him. In a few years, he will probably follow the legacies of Stephon Marbury and Steve Francis, point guards from the early 2000's, who are just as well-known for their careers' spectacular crashes as they are for their actual play, or even their inclination to win ball games.

NBA analysts have said this of Westbrook ever since he made the leap to superstar status. Such claims are not totally without merit. Westbrook will sometimes try to do too much. In Game 2 of the 2012 NBA Finals against the Miami Heat, Westbrook took 27 shots in comparison to 22 shots from Durant. However, despite taking more shots, Westbrook finished with only 26 points as compared to 32 for Durant. The great Magic Johnson, who won five NBA titles, said, "That was the worst point guard in a championship series I have ever seen." In the aftermath of the James Harden trade and Harden's subsequent explosion to NBA superstardom, some analysts wonder whether Oklahoma City would have been better off trading Westbrook for another point guard, with someone who would emphasize passing the ball instead of taking difficult shots.

Despite the criticisms, the Thunder appreciated Westbrook's talent. Whenever Durant becomes more passive, or when the better defenses in the league swarm him, Westbrook is right there to clean up. His athleticism and scoring mentality allow him to take over a game in a way that a pass-first point guard cannot. Westbrook, along with Durant, created one of the most lethal offensive combinations, if not the best duo, in the entire NBA. It was when Westbrook made the leap to becoming an NBA All-Star that the Thunders transitioned from just another playoff team to real contenders. As Oklahoma City continues the chase for their first championship, Kevin Durant is unquestionably their leader. Even Jordan needed his Pippen, though, and the Thunders will need Westbrook, a star in his right, to fight, hustle, and make those difficult shots that he often takes. It is something that he has done over and over again in his rising, but never comfortable, basketball career.

And though Durant has been heralded as the clear go-to guy of the OKC Thunder in his stint with the team, one might question if KD is even the best player on the Thunder roster. Russell Westbrook has become so good at every facet of the game that many have come to think that the Oklahoma City Thunder is his team instead of Durant's. When Durant was saddled with injury for most of the 2014-15 season, Russell Westbrook became an absolute beast on the hard court. With no scoring option in the Thunder lineup other than Dion Waiters and Enes Kanter, Westbrook took it upon himself to carry the scoring load that KD left. He was so good in scoring and doing everything possible that he became a triple-double machine, the NBA's scoring champion, and an MVP candidate.

In those stretches, Russell Westbrook was nigh impossible to stop as a player and was racking up numbers that even someone like LeBron James could not contend with. That was indeed Westbrook's coming out party as a legitimate NBA superstar, and people saw a glimpse of what he could do if he carried a team singlehandedly. And when KD came back from injury, questions arose about whether the two could coexist and whether a falling out period would occur, much like what happened with Kobe Bryant and Shaquille O'Neal way back. However, nothing of the sorts has happened thus far, and Westbrook and Durant have been playing together with unmatchable chemistry.

Thinking back to the time when the OKC Thunder drafted Russell Westbrook as the 5th overall pick in the 2008 NBA Draft, the former UCLA shooting guard, who has turned into one of the best point guards in the NBA, has become a multiple-time All-Star. He has been an All-Star game MVP, a multiple-time All-NBA Team member, and an NBA scoring champion. While a lot of people have doubted his ability to play at that position or alongside Kevin Durant, he has since proved all his doubters wrong and is on pace to turning OKC into serious championship contenders once again.

Chapter 1: Childhood and Early Life

On November 12, 1988, Russell Westbrook III was born to Russell Westbrook, Sr. and Shannon Horton of Long Beach, California. Growing up in Compton with a father who idolized Magic Johnson, Westbrook was introduced to basketball at the age of 7. Russell Sr. was a playground legend in Los Angeles and was the best person to learn from in the case of the younger Russell.[i] Soon after, Westbrook began tagging along with his father to Ross Snyder Park, a run-down shack at the intersection of 41st and Compton Avenue. Basketball, as well as guidance from his parents, helped keep Westbrook off the rough streets of Los Angeles. His father served time for a drug charge after Westbrook's birth and vowed never to return to prison. This conviction was reinforced after Russell Westbrook Sr. watched one of his old friends get gunned down on the street. While a lot of NBA superstars grew up with broken families and a lot of bad influence from the streets, Russell Westbrook was fortunate to have a father who was always there for him and a mother who kept her sons away from the negativities of society.

Westbrook's father began taking him to Jesse Owens Park, a small gym in Los Angeles. His father introduced him to Reggie Hamilton, who coached a traveling basketball team known as the L.A. Elite. When the young Westbrook requested a roster spot, Hamilton happily obliged. Hamilton noted Westbrook's competitive spirit and shared this observation with The Oklahoman later, saying, "He did not like to lose, and he definitely always played hard. So that was a good, positive thing right off the bat."[ii]

Unfortunately, not everything was positive for Westbrook at the time. "He could not shoot a lick," Hamilton said, adding that, "If Russell made a shot back then, it was just a bonus." Today, a display case of photos hanging on the wall just inside the gym at Jesse Owens Park still has a picture of 10-year-old Westbrook. Hamilton recalls Westbrook playing with the same emotion back then as he displays now in the NBA. "He was way more emotional then," Hamilton said. He added, "Russell would go out there and cry if he was going through some problems."[iii]

In addition to Hamilton, Russell Sr. was one of the driving forces behind Westbrook's success. Hours upon hours were spent together at the gym. Westbrook would shoot five hundred shots a day, often practicing until his arms hurt and his legs gave out. Despite the physical burden, Westbrook never complained. Whenever he was gasping for breath, or his body was on the brink of exhaustion, his father would motivate and assure him. His father would always tell him that if he worked hard enough, he would be able to earn a college scholarship.

The family would later move to Hawthorne, a city near LA, when Russell was 12 years old. Westbrook would go to school at Leuzinger High School where he started playing a more organized style of basketball.

Chapter 2: High School Years

As a freshman at Leuzinger High School, Westbrook stood at just 5'8". At the time, he so lacked in athleticism that he could not even dunk until his junior year. His coach even described him once as "deathly slow" in his first year in high school. However, what Westbrook lacked in size at the time, he made up with guts. One day, Westbrook's high school coach, Reggie Morris, threw Westbrook into a rebounding drill with his varsity squad, which boasted six players who were 6'5" or taller. Westbrook held his own against his teammates with little more than a pair of freakishly long arms and hands that could already palm entire basketballs.

Westbrook's heart and toughness were not just shown on the court. When he was not practicing at the Leuzinger High School gym, Westbrook's father would drive him to practice at Rowley Park, which was five minutes away. Westbrook shot jumpers, practiced calisthenics, and even practiced on Thanksgiving Day. Russ spent more time in Rowley than in his high school's gym because he could work on his game more effectively with the supervision of his father than he could in high school, where the coaches focused more on developing the older players and seniors.

However, despite his hard work, Westbrook did not make the varsity team until his junior year. In the summer before his senior year, the only schools willing to offer Westbrook a scholarship were better known for their academics than for their athletics.[iv] Things began looking up in Westbrook's senior year. The short Westbrook finally underwent a growth spurt, reaching a height of 6'2" and finished high school at 6'3". With the departure of the upperclassmen that dominated the team before him, Westbrook became the primary focus of the Leuzinger basketball team. He took full advantage of the opportunity. In his senior year, Westbrook averaged 25 points and nine rebounds per game, while leading Leuzinger to an impressive 25-4 record. Westbrook was just as competitive off the court as he was on it. He wanted his grades to be just as good as his basketball skills. At the same time, he would also go after the prettiest girls in his class.

As Westbrook showed his potential in his senior year, Division I college basketball programs such as Wake Forest, Kansas, and UCLA all tried to recruit him. UCLA, in particular, wanted Westbrook to fill the vacant spot on their roster when Jordan Farmar declared his intention to join the 2006 NBA Draft. While Westbrook initially felt that a roster as strong as UCLA would not give him an opportunity to show that he was a star,

Westbrook's parents wanted him to graduate from UCLA, and it was a school very close to home. Out of respect for his parents' wishes, Westbrook decided to join the UCLA Bruins in 2006.

Chapter 3: College Years at UCLA

Freshman Year

While UCLA decided to give Westbrook a scholarship, the reality was that no one knew what to expect from him. Westbrook had never played Amateur Athletic Union (AAU) ball, where all of the best high school basketball players in the United States compete against each other. He had never been nominated to the McDonald's All-American Team and had very little high school pedigree aside from a strong senior season, and was not particularly skilled. He was athletic and hard-working, but plenty of college basketball players with those traits had failed over the years. Thus, there was uncertainty about whether Westbrook would be able to stay on the team, especially on a roster like UCLA's, which was filled with future NBA players like Arron Afflalo, Luc Richard Mbah a Moute, and Darren Collison. With Darren Collison as the team's starting point guard and Afflalo playing most of the shooting guard duties, Russell Westbrook was relegated as a bench player.

For the most part, Westbrook's freshman year was rather pedestrian. He was a highly athletic player, but his jump shot and ball handling skills were still shaky. Thus, UCLA coach,

Ben Howland, had Westbrook function as an energy player instead of as the star that he would soon become. Westbrook started with only one game as a freshman in 2007. He played only 9 minutes per game with an average score of 3.4 points per game. At that time, Westbrook did not reflect the same player that would be drafted 4th in the next NBA Draft. He could not even get more than 10 minutes a game and was not even a difference-maker for the Bruins, let alone a future NBA superstar.

It was Westbrook's hard work and perseverance that made him rise to the top. As Westbrook's freshman year drew to a close, the coaching staff encouraged him to work on his all-around game and concentrate on his jump shot. However, the coaching staff apparently said similar words to every returning player, and no one expected Westbrook to improve as rapidly as he did. Back then, NCAA rules prevented coaches from having any interaction with their players during the summer. As Donaldson remembered, the UCLA coaching staff could only listen while reviews of Westbrook's games with the elite, NBA-level talent in the Men's Gym poured in. "In those games, guys do not want to get embarrassed. There is a minimal amount of defense being played. Most of the guys are working on their jumper. Russell, every time he got the ball... he would take it to the hole and try to dunk."

Even those who knew nothing about evaluating talent noticed something different in Westbrook's game. Ryan Finney, men's basketball sports information director, saw a profound maturity in his game. He stated, "I remember saying to some of our assistants that he had really progressed. I do not have the coaching background, but from what I saw, he was not afraid." Westbrook's game had slowed down. While he remained an athletic force, he was not the hyperactive, confused player they had seen before.

Sophomore Year

Westbrook came into his sophomore year with the UCLA Bruins as a more developed and more mature individual. Furthermore, as the 2007-2008 college basketball season began, opportunity knocked on Westbrook's front door. At the start of the season, the Bruins' starting point guard, Darren Collison, strained his MCL, which is a severe knee injury. Coach Howland had no choice but to start Westbrook. Another development that transpired was that a new freshman, future NBA superstar Kevin Love, had joined UCLA. Love was amazed by Westbrook's continued drive and hard work.

One day, Love showed up at the gym at an early hour to get some pre-practice workouts in, only to find Westbrook already there, sweat pouring off of his brow. By the time Love finished, Westbrook was still going. The two future superstars worked together admirably, and the Bruins won their first seven games while Collison recovered. When Collison returned, Howland decided to move Westbrook to the shooting guard position, and at one point, even benched him for five games to see how the roster would fit. Westbrook was jolted around from position to position, role to role, but he never complained. He understood that the coach was doing what was necessary to create the best fit for the Bruins. As a starter, Russell Westbrook's role was mostly to play defense because he had the apparent athleticism and the ferocity to work hard on that end of the floor.

With his minutes and role significantly increased, Westbrook's numbers soared. In his sophomore year, he averaged 12.7 points per game, 3.9 rebounds per game, and 4.3 assists per game. The assists total was almost certainly the most impressive of all. Considering Westbrook spent most of his sophomore year playing off the ball while Collison played point guard, he was still able to lead UCLA in assists per game. The UCLA Bruins made the NCAA Final Four where they lost to the University of Memphis 78-63 led by Derrick Rose, another athletic point guard who was regarded as the best NBA prospect and who was much better than Russell. Although Memphis scored 53 points between future NBA players Chris Douglas-Roberts and Derrick Rose, Westbrook still managed 22 points in the defeat. Shortly afterward, Westbrook was awarded the Pac-10 Defensive Player of the Year award, while at the same time, also making the All-Pac-10 Third Team.

While UCLA had lost in the end, Westbrook had gained in a huge way with his impressive sophomore season. Back in 2007, very few NBA teams even knew who Westbrook was, much less considered drafting him. Now with his improvement, every team in the draft lottery knew him. NBA teams were intrigued by his upsides, his defensive capability, and his hard work ethics. While he was a good player in college, he was not a pure point guard and played mostly as the shooting guard. Nevertheless, he had enough talent to make it into the NBA as a role player or as a sparkplug for the offense. Westbrook had gone from a complete unknown to a possible lottery pick or a top 15 draft choice. Thus, after UCLA's elimination in the Final Four, he decided to declare his intention for the 2008 NBA Draft. It was an incredible transition for a player who had not been highly coveted in his high school years and had been a college bench player just one year earlier.

Chapter 4: Russell's NBA Career

Getting Drafted

In the 2008 NBA Draft, there was no doubt that Derrick Rose was the consensus top draft pick. The point guard out of Memphis was big and very athletic for his position. Moreover, his playmaking skills and ability to score were at a level far above his draft peers. There was another prospect in the draft that did not get as much attention as Rose, though. A kid by the name of Russell Westbrook was just as athletic and as big as Rose was. Sadly, at that point in his life, Russ just did not have the skills or the natural point guard abilities that Rose had. Moreover, for a shooting guard, Westbrook was small at just 6'3".

Nevertheless, Westbrook was still a very promising player entering the NBA Draft. As a tweener who could player either the point guard or the shooting guard positions, Russell Westbrook was compared to Monta Ellis. Ellis was another one of those small athletic guards that could score at will with his speed and finishing ability. Ellis was more of a shooting guard than a point guard because of his mentality of scoring first before making plays. As young and inexperienced as he was, Westbrook was exactly the type of player that Ellis was.

The young combo guard was regarded by a lot of scouts as a player on top of the list purely concerning athleticism. He had the speed, quickness, and explosiveness that was unseen from players his size. Offensively, Westbrook was almost unstoppable when he decided to go to the basket. He always had that quick crossover move or first step that could get easily get him to the basket. When attacking the rim, Russell could absorb contact and mix it up with the paint defenders because he had a finishing ability that complemented his strong jumping abilities. Though not a pure point guard, Westbrook led UCLA in assists, and it was a testament to his passing ability, although it was not the best part of his game.[v]

There have been a lot of 6'3" players with the athleticism of Russell Westbrook. What set Russ apart from those players was the fact that he played with a lot of energy and intensity on the floor. Not only did he make it a point to run on transition on every play, but he also focused a lot of his energy to limiting the fast breaks and defending his man as well.[vi]

Defensively, Russell Westbrook was never a slacker. He always poured in as much energy on that end of the floor as he did on offense, if not more. With a wingspan of more than 6'7", Russell made up for his height of only 6'3", and that arm length allowed him to defend players bigger than he is. And with his freakish athleticism, Westbrook could stay with his man for the whole stretch of the game.[vii] No wonder he was Pac-10 Defensive Player of the Year.

As good and athletic he is, Westbrook was still very raw and unpolished entering the NBA Draft. While Rose already had a smooth offensive game that could get him open layups and pull-up jumpers on the perimeter, Westbrook's offensive game was predicated more on his athletic ability than his skills on that side of the floor. Russell Westbrook had a very questionable jump shot, even after staying for two years in UCLA. Though he had a lot of lift when he shot his jumpers, his mechanics were still not there when it came to his release and precision. As such, he did not have the ability to create his shots off the dribble. This was a huge turnoff for a lot of NBA teams because the guard position should be polished regarding shooting mechanics. Aside from his inability to shoot, Russ was also a mediocre ball handler, and it prevented him from playing point guard for heavy minutes.[viii]

Much like Ellis, Russell Westbrook was never regarded as a "true point guard." He did play point guard when Collison was injured, but was relegated to the shooting guard position for most of the season. Aside from his inability to handle the ball at a high level, another thing that made him unable to play the point guard position effectively was his mindset. Westbrook always thought of attacking the basket every time he had the ball in his hands. Point guards always made it a point to make plays for other people, even if they had the attacking skills of a Russell Westbrook. Meanwhile, Westbrook was a bull in a china shop when he decided to go to the basket. He was reckless, and he did not care about anything else going on the floor.[ix]

With all those things in mind, DraftExpress.com slated Westbrook as a possible lottery pick. However, he was described as a tweener, someone who did not have a stable playing position and would often bounce between two posts. In Westbrook's case, he did not have the mentality or the ball handling ability to play the point guard position, but also did not have the size or the shooting touch to play shooting guard. As such, he was also described as someone who could be a role player at the NBA level. Something scouts and experts did not take into account, though, was Russell Westbrook's unmatched work ethic.

While Westbrook was slated to be a lottery pick or a player who could be chosen just outside of the top 10, draft scouts remained concerned about his shooting, as well as the fact that his rise was too meteoric. Their concern was the possibility that Westbrook's sophomore year, amazing as it was, was just a fluke and was predicated more on UCLA's lack of guards instead of Westbrook's skills. In 13 mock drafts compiled by sports organizations like ESPN and Sports Illustrated in the days before the NBA Draft, not a single one had Westbrook being selected in the top 5. In fact, one had him being chosen as low as 12.

However, the Seattle SuperSonics had different plans with the fourth overall pick. They badly needed a point guard, and as a rebuilding team, they were more than willing to wait for Westbrook to develop into a star, or at the very least, an accomplished starter who could help usher a new era. They were also impressed by Westbrook's heart and work ethics when they saw him participate in draft workout after draft workout with practically no rest.

On June 26, 2008, Derrick Rose came out as the top draft choice, as expected. Next came Michael Beasley, who was also projected to be drafted behind Rose especially because of polished offensive game. The shooter OJ May was chosen third behind Rose and Beasley. Then the Seattle SuperSonics drafted Westbrook with the 4th pick. As Westbrook walked to the stage, shook hands with NBA Commissioner David Stern, and donned the green hat of the Sonics, Jay Bilas observed, "Who would have thought last year, at this time, that Russell Westbrook would have been the fourth pick in this draft?"

Despite this, many around the league felt that drafting Westbrook was a risky move, having been selected over more established college stars such as Jerryd Bayless, the Lopez twins, and fellow UCLA teammate, forward Kevin Love. Any of those players could have been a "better" choice than Westbrook because the Sonics were still a rebuilding team, and they were missing key pieces at virtually every position other than small forward.

The consensus was that several teams in the draft lottery would be interested in Westbrook later on, and many argued that Westbrook should have been the top draft choice as judged by his current NBA career, but no one could have predicted he would have gone as high as number 4 pick overall. Still, the city believed in him. They saw a young man with a burning desire to strive for perfection constantly. He was an outstanding defensive talent with uncanny instincts as a player. They saw him as the kind of player who could manage the front line, both offensively and defensively.

Westbrook may have worn the hat of the Sonics, but he would never play for Seattle. A few months afterward, the Sonics would move to Oklahoma City and rename themselves the

Thunder. Oklahoma City had received their first sports franchise, and while it was understood that the Thunder would be undergoing a developing year, the fans remained enthusiastic about their new team. Russell Westbrook would become one of the few players to be part of the Sonic's final NBA Draft.

Rookie Season

During the 2008-2009 season, Westbrook's rookie year, Oklahoma City had three intriguing prospects in Durant, Westbrook, and fellow high pick, Jeff Green. They also saw the potential of a stout big man in Nick Collison. The rest of the team was filled with players who barely belonged in the league, though. Aside from the four players mentioned above, not a single player that played more than 25 games on the 2008-2009 team is still in the league five seasons later. With no veteran talent on the floor, the young Russell Westbrook was given the duty to play as the point guard for the Thunder. He would also start at that position for the majority of his rookie season. Moreover, the OKC Thunder were still adjusting to their relocation from Seattle. They were also a rebuilding team picking up the pieces from their Seattle days when they had chosen to trade star players Ray Allen and Rashard Lewis in order to get younger talent. It was going to be a rough season, and Westbrook's start in the NBA did not begin smoothly.

In his NBA debut against the Milwaukee Bucks, Westbrook scored 13 points. At the beginning of the season, his raw numbers seemed fine for a rookie. However, his scoring percentages were dreadful as he shot 34.5% for the month of November, including three games where he shot less than 17%. While Westbrook was an athletic specimen, his ability to adjust to the even more athletic NBA was put into question.

After that dismal November, Westbrook showed that he did have the capacity to adapt to the NBA. On November 22, 2008, the Thunder fired head coach P.J. Carlesimo after losing ten straight games and replaced him with Scott Brooks. Brooks had never been a head coach before, but as an NBA player, he had won a championship as part of the 1994 Houston Rockets. The Thunder and Westbrook responded positively to the coaching change.

Westbrook, in particular, roared back in December. He shot 46% for the month, which is a high number for any point guard, and more so for a rookie. On December 6, Westbrook scored a career high of 30 points against the Miami Heat. Three weeks later, he broke his career high again by scoring 31 points against the Phoenix Suns. Westbrook received the Western Conference Rookie of the Month award, and in early January, ESPN columnist John Hollinger wrote that while the Rookie of the

Year race had turned into a competition between two other scoring-first guards, OJ Mayo and Derrick Rose, Russell Westbrook's numbers were just as good as the two of them.

NBA teams began to pay more attention to guarding Westbrook out of respect for his great month, and he never played quite as well as he did that December. Despite the lack of help, Westbrook continued to put forth a strong rookie year. He scored a new career high of 34 points against the Sacramento Kings in February and hit 20 free throws, the most ever made by a player opposing the Kings since the team's move to Sacramento in 1984. Westbrook was nominated for the Western Conference Rookie of the Month award yet again in February, and then promptly showed that he deserved it by grabbing his first career triple-double against the Dallas Mavericks with 17 points, ten assists, and ten rebounds. He was the first rookie since Chris Paul to grab a triple double. As rookies go, a triple-double seems to be a rarity, especially for point guards.

Despite his glaring inconsistency as a scoring point guard, Russell Westbrook was already displaying his versatility as early as his rookie year in the NBA. Russ could drive and score the ball with his relentless attacking mentality while also showing his ability to set teammates up for scoring opportunities. He could also grab rebounds at a high rate while showing a lot of intensity on the defensive end of the court. His ability to play all facets of the game helped him compile ten double-doubles for the season.

As the 2008-2009 season came to an end, the Oklahoma City Thunder did not have much to be proud of from a team standpoint in the regular season. They finished with a 23-59 record, an improvement of a mere three games from the previous year, and had the third-worst record in the league. But even that 23-59 record was an improvement when you look back and see where the Thunder had started, going 3-29 to start the season. Westbrook had shown that he deserved to be picked fourth after all. Furthermore, Westbrook silenced the doubters that said that he could never play point guard in the NBA. Russell Westbrook displayed one of the quickest and smoothest transitions from college shooting guard to NBA point guard.

At the end of his rookie season, Russell Westbrook averaged 15.3 points, 5.3 assists, and 4.9 rebounds, and was placed on the All-Rookie First Team. His numbers were even better than what he averaged in his final year with UCLA. It was a testament of how quick Russ was blooming with his unbelievable work ethic. While Derrick Rose would win the Rookie of the Year Award, Westbrook placed fourth overall in the voting and received two first-place votes. His numbers were not even far from Rose, though he was playing with an established future star in Durant.

However, Russell Westbrook's rookie season did not end without any criticism on the part of the UCLA product. For someone who was playing the point guard position and was supposed to be a playmaker for a more established scorer in the 2008 reigning Rookie of the Year Kevin Durant, Westbrook took a lot of shots at about 13 attempts per game. The problem did not lie in the number of shots he was taking, but it was in the quality of his efforts. Westbrook, instead of passing the ball over to Durant or Green, took a lot of ill-advised shots in his rookie season to the detriment of his team. And with his raw jump shot and less-than-mediocre perimeter game at that time, he shot a little below 40% from the floor.

Russell Westbrook was also dreadfully turnover-prone in his rookie season. Not only was he taking a lot of ill-advised attempts from the floor but was also out of control on most plays. Even when the numbers were not in the Thunder's favor during the transition and even when the lane was shut down, Russ would relentlessly and recklessly attack the basket only to turn his journeys into turnovers or bad shots. The hothead from UCLA apparently needed a lot of maturity if he wanted to become a star in the league.

Despite the flaws that Westbrook was showing, it was expected of a rookie to perform sub-par. But, for Westbrook's case, he exceeded expectations despite the glaring weaknesses in his game early on in his career. Nobody expected him to have a productive rookie season, but everyone knew that Oklahoma City Thunder still had a few more years to develop, and it was clear that they had a great competitive core in Westbrook and Durant to build around.

Sophomore Year

With a young and developing core, the OKC Thunder were off to a good future, especially with Kevin Durant and Russell Westbrook leading their charge. With their very young and talented roster, the front office did not care to make any significant offseason moves, even with their relatively high cap space. The best that they did before the season was drafting James Harden as the 3rd overall pick and made a trade to get the rookie point guard Eric Maynor. Harden was also a questionable choice considering that he was merely a three-point shooter and an un-athletic player at that point in his career, and considering that there were several other talented players available, like the eventual Rookie of the Year Tyreke Evans, future two-time MVP Stephen Curry, and athletic wingman DeMar DeRozan. Nonetheless, they stuck with Harden since they thought he could help usher in a brighter future for the Thunder in a few years.

As it turned out, the Thunder did not need to wait much longer for that bright future. In their 2009-2010 season preview, a panel of ESPN experts predicted that the Thunder would finish 11th in the West, with not a single expert predicting them to make it into the playoffs. Even ESPN columnist Bill Simmons, who correctly predicted that Kevin Durant would win the scoring title in 2009-10, only gave a prediction of 42 wins for the Thunder. While improving to 42 games after winning 23 games the previous season would have been impressive enough, the Thunder exploded in 2009-2010. The Thunder finished with 50 wins, becoming the youngest team in NBA history to win so many games. They would also make it to the NBA playoffs for the first time since 2004-2005, back when they were still known as the Seattle SuperSonics.

How did the Thunder turn around so dramatically? A great deal of the credit went to Kevin Durant, who won the scoring title, averaging the highest points per game in the league and making his first All-Star Team as well as the All-NBA First Team. But in addition to Durant, Russell Westbrook matured dramatically as a player and full-time starting point guard. While he had scored well enough as a rookie, his passing had left something to be desired.

Westbrook worked in the off-season on his ball handling and passing skills and the improved talent around the Thunder meant that Westbrook's passes were now more likely to end up in actual assists. In his sophomore year, Westbrook's assists shot up from 5.3 to 8 per game. He accomplished this while not increasing his turnovers, a common trade-off when an NBA player's assist numbers rise. Westbrook was very improved as a player and was one of the brightest young stars in the NBA. It all started when Westbrook shocked the world by making 23 total assists in his first two games that season to help the Thunder get a 2-0 start.

While Westbrook's passing improved, he remained a capable scoring threat. In Oklahoma City's fifth game of the season, Westbrook scored 33 points in a losing effort against the Houston Rockets. Despite the loss, he bounced back well by putting up 17 points and ten assists in their 28-point win effort against the Orlando Magic the next game.

If Russell Westbrook's playmaking improvements were not shocking enough, what was even more shocking was his growing unselfishness. On December 2 against the Philadelphia 76ers, despite shooting 1 out of 11 from the floor, Westbrook delivered 15 passes that turned into assists for his teammates. Was that the moment that Russ legitimately transformed into a point guard? One would usually think so.

Immediately after only scoring 7 points when he dished out 15 assists, Westbrook's improvement on his scoring consistency was also on display as he put up a 13-game streak of double-digit point production. In that span of games, he never forgot to make plays for teammates as he had three double-doubles. More importantly, the Thunder only lost six games during that stretch. Had that been a year ago, they would have only won three out of those 13 games.

Continuing to improve on an unexpectedly impressive rookie season, Russell Westbrook's focus that season was not about making the jump in scoring but rather in making himself an even better point guard after playing the off guard for the majority of his formative years in basketball. After only ten double-digit assist games in his rookie season, Russell broke that mark as early as January 13, 2010, when he delivered 13 dimes along with 25 points in an overtime losing effort to the San Antonio Spurs.

After impressive performances in the first half of the season heading into the All-Star Weekend, Westbrook still was not an All-Star at that point in his career, but he was nevertheless the brightest young star in the Rookie Challenge. Joining the sophomore squad against the rookie team, Westbrook bullied his way to 40 big points as he was nigh unstoppable in that game. However, his big performance was not enough to help his team beat the rookies, who won by 12.

Russell Westbrook would use the momentum of his stellar performance in the All-Star Weekend to perform better than he ever had in his two-year career and to give the Thunder their much-needed push at that crucial juncture of the season as they were seeking a spot in the playoffs. First off, Russ would have his second career triple-double by putting up 22 points, ten rebounds, and 14 assists in a win over the Minnesota Timberwolves. Eleven of Russell Westbrook's 24 double-digit assist games came after the All-Star break as the Thunder won 20 of their final 31 games to push themselves to a 50-win season.

While his scoring average improved from 15.3 to 16.1 points per game in the 2009-10 season, his maturity, though improved, was still something to be worked on. Some people questioned whether Westbrook was too fast for his own good because there were a lot of instances where he would play out of control. He would still attack the basket recklessly and without even thinking of what to do when he got there. In those instances, he would often turn the ball over or put up an ill-advised shot.

Those mistakes led Coach Scott Brooks to bench him in critical situations and opted to play the pass-first and more in-control rookie point guard Eric Maynor instead. However, those were seemingly simple growing pains for the maturing Russell Westbrook. He did help the Thunder win the 8th seed in the ultra-competitive Western Conference with 50 wins in the season, a drastic improvement from the previous season.

If you thought he already reached his sophomore peak in the regular season, it was in fact in the playoffs when Westbrook showed what he was capable of. As the 8th seed, the Thunder had to face the top-seeded defending champions the Los Angeles Lakers in the first round. The Lakers had one of the best guards ever to play the game in Kobe Bryant, but their primary advantage was their All-Star frontcourt stars, Pau Gasol and Andrew Bynum, versus their weak Thunder frontcourt counterparts, rookie Serge Ibaka, Nick Collison, and Nenad Kristić.

On the other hand, while Durant would be covered by elite perimeter defender Ron Artest (now known as Metta World Peace), Westbrook would be faced up against Derek Fisher, a 36-year-old point guard who, in the last playoffs, had struggled to defend other scoring point guards like Aaron Brooks and Chauncey Billups. The aging Derek Fisher, though a good defender in his prime, was deemed too slow at that point in his career. If Oklahoma City had any hope of pulling off the upset, then Westbrook would need to eviscerate Fisher throughout the entire series with his superior speed and athleticism.

Westbrook did just that. In Game 1 of the NBA Playoffs, Westbrook scored 23 points against the Lakers and also had eight assists and four rebounds. Although the Thunder would lose that game to the Lakers 79 to 87, it was evident that neither Derek Fisher nor the other Laker point guard could guard Russell Westbrook. The Lakers would win another game in Los Angeles despite the tough fight put up by OKC to grab a 2-0 lead in the series.

In Game 3, in front of a raucous Oklahoma City crowd giddy to see their Thunder in the playoffs, Westbrook scored 27 points on Fisher to yet again make minced meat out of the old veteran's defense. While the Lakers' defense focused heavily on Durant, limiting him to 35% shooting for the series, Westbrook feasted on the Lakers and took full advantage of the pressure on Durant. Meanwhile, KD defended Kobe and limited him to 10 out of 29 shooting from the field, and the OKC Thunder won a shocker in Oklahoma, 101-96. The Thunder would pull off another upset over the Lakers in Game 4. This time, it was a 110 to 89 thrashing led by KD's 22 and Westbrook's 18 points. Kobe took only ten shots the entire game against the tough defense of Durant.

Laker head coach Phil Jackson made the necessary adjustment in Game 5. Knowing that no other guard on the Lakers roster could keep up with Russell Westbrook, he decided to have Kobe Bryant, one of the best perimeter defenders in NBA history, to guard Russ. With Kobe focused on defense, Westbrook could not even put up a shot and was limited to only 4 out of 13 for 15 points. KD only had 17, and the Laker frontline dominated the Thunder as Gasol and Bynum combined for 46 points. With Kobe on Westbrook in Game 6, the young point guard was again severely limited to just 7 out of 20 from the field in a game that the Thunder would have won if not for a putback made by Pau Gasol to finally eliminate the young and pesky Oklahoma City Thunder.

Though the Thunder would lose the series, their first since relocating to Oklahoma, in an impressive 6-game performance, Westbrook would average 20.5 points with 47% shooting and six assists. Westbrook also turned up his perimeter defense, averaging 1.7 steals for the series. While it was disappointing for the Thunder to be out in the first round, they had performed valiantly against the defending champions, the Lakers, who would go on to win their second straight title. Who knew how good they could be the next year?

Over the previous two seasons, Westbrook had shown the potential to become one of the top point guards in the league. His passing had improved, his understanding of the intricacies of the pick-and-roll game (one of the main Thunder weapons in the half-court game) had gotten better, and he had performed extremely well in his first playoff series. While his draft rival Derrick Rose became an All-Star in his second season, it was only a matter of time until Westbrook would reach that level and become an All-Star as well.

Rise to All-Stardom

Banking on their very impressive first-round encounter against the eventual back-to-back champions, the Oklahoma City Thunder came into the 2010-11 season with a lot of enthusiasm and optimism that their team would only get better as their core stars developed. Again, the Thunder did not do much to improve their lineup coming into the new season because they were banking on the development of their draft choices. Kevin Durant was molding into the best scorer in the NBA, and Russell Westbrook was steadily using his natural abilities to make himself a force to be reckoned with.

As part of his mission to prove critics wrong, Russell Westbrook's rise to the level of an All-Star that season coincided with the massive improvements to the way the Oklahoma City Thunder played. While most would attribute that to Kevin Durant's scoring greatness, Russell Westbrook's continued evolution was just as vital to the cause of the Thunder, as was the points that KD was putting up on the board. Westbrook provided what Durant could not: energy.

From the start of the season, nobody could dismiss how valuable Westbrook's relentless assault and seemingly unrivaled energy was. While KD was the stabilizer on offense because of his unparalleled ability to put the ball through the hoop, Westbrook brought the flamethrower whenever the offense was cold with stagnancy. When you had Durant checked by some of the best wing defenders in the league, Russ was there to clean the mess up and provide the offense.

Westbrook would open the 2010-11 season with a matchup against the Chicago Bulls and his draft mate Derrick Rose, who was seen as having the same athletic abilities, but was much better and more in control of his game. However, Russ was the better of the two at that one night. While the two future superstars would score 28 points each, Russell Westbrook had ten rebounds and six assists to lead his team to a victory that night. And, with a 17-point 11-assist performance against Detroit two days later, the Thunder started the season 2-0.

Russell Westbrook's unfathomable relentlessness in attacking the basket had become more evident that season as he continued to drive to the basket and get foul attempts by the dozen. On November 12, 2010, Westbrook had 36 points on 12 out of 22 shooting while also making 11 of his 12 foul line attempts in a win versus the Portland Trailblazers. Just two nights before, he had 31 points on 9 out of 11 shooting from the charity stripe to go along with 12 assists against the Philadelphia 76ers. And when he scored 31 points on 11 out of 13 shooting from the 15-point line, the league was put on notice that Westbrook's only purpose was to attack and attack.

Westbrook's attacking mentality bore its most fruitful output early that season when the spitfire guard out of UCLA manhandled the Indiana Pacers' defense on November 26. Armed with nothing but his vicious assault to the basket, Westbrook destroyed the Pacers for a then career-best 43 points on 13 out of 24 shooting. His most impressive stat that game was his 17 of his 18 made attempts from the charity stripe. If that performance was not enough, he did the same to the New Jersey Nets barely a week later when he had a near triple-double of 38 points, 15 rebounds, and nine assists.

It was in 2011 that Westbrook's potential showed itself, as he transformed into one of the very best point guards in the game. His passing had improved in 2009-10. In 2010-11, Westbrook's scoring, always his bread and butter, became evident as he averaged 24 points per game in November 2010. He won the Player of the Week award in November because of his improved scoring abilities. Westbrook continued to score above 20 points per game night in and night out. He was showing improved maturity on the court and was rarely playing out of control.

Because defenders were becoming more wary about this fiery point guard's ability to put the roof on fire, Russell Westbrook's scoring took a slight dip in December. However, his ability to control the tempo and contribute in all facets of the game did not take a vacation. In that month, Westbrook had a total of five double-doubles, which included his first triple-double effort that season on December 31 just as the year was about to end. He had 23 points, ten rebounds, and ten assists in that win against the Atlanta Hawks. On the other hand, the Thunder would only lose five of their 16 assignments in December.

The New Year was even better for Westbrook as he put together five straight games of assisting on at least ten baskets. He even had a triple-double, his second of the season, on January 13,

2011, when he had 32 points, ten rebounds, and 13 assists versus the Orlando Magic. In his very next game, he had 32 points and 12 assists to go for back-to-back 30-10 games. Wrapping off a productive January was another triple-double. He had 35 points, 13 rebounds, and 13 assists in a win over the Washington Wizards on January 28. With those kinds of performances, Westbrook became the embodiment of an all-around point guard. He could defend, pass, rebound, and score with the best of them.

What made him an even better scorer that season was that Westbrook added a new facet to his game—the pull-up jump shot. While shooting was regarded as his weakness, Russ erased that notion and improved that aspect of his game to make the perimeter shot one of his best weapons. His blinding speed kept his defenders sagging on him and guard for his ability to blow by and go to the rim. Westbrook used that to his advantage. Knowing that defenders would give him space as he tried to drive, he would suddenly halt his movement and rise to shoot a jump shot while his defender was on his heel, unable to contest the shot. His pull-up jumper was regarded as a tough shot considering how hard it is to suddenly stop on a dime after moving with such blinding speed. Russell Westbrook also improved his three-point shooting from being a low 20%

shooter to shooting 33% from that area. He suddenly became a complete offensive juggernaut.

What made Westbrook an improved jump shooter that season was that he fixed his release mechanics. Russ, in his younger years, always had a beautiful form from toe to hand. He could jump high enough to see over the defenders whenever he set himself up for a jumper. Westbrook could then release his shot at the apex of his jump to make the most of the height and the momentum that his legs gave him. However, what was thoroughly wrong about his release was that he was pointing his shooting arm's elbow outside instead of pointing it square to the basket.[x]

But in his third year in the league, the broken release turned into a finesse and beautiful rhythm shot off the bounce. Westbrook learned how to keep his elbow tucked while also learning how to properly guide his shot using the off-hand.[x] Through repetition and hard work, he has learned how to do that shot effortlessly off the dribble to turn it into a reliable weapon whenever his driving lanes got cut off.

With Westbrook playing at a very high level, coaches and teams suddenly turned their attentions to OKC's budding star. In February, he was nominated to his first All-Star game alongside his two-time All-Star teammate Kevin Durant. Held at Los

Angeles' Staples Center, Westbrook saw billboards of himself posted in his hometown city. In his midseason classic debut, Russell Westbrook played extremely efficiently in just 14 minutes by scoring 12 points. Not bad for a 22-year-old first-timer in the All-Star game.

The excitement of having two legitimate All-Stars in Kevin Durant and Russell Westbrook had also benefited the Thunder's quest for a playoff spot. With Durant scoring his usual numbers and Westbrook feeding off the energy of his first trip to the midseason classic, the dynamic duo would lead the Thunder to a record of 20-8 in their final 28 games after the All-Star break to become one of the top contenders in a harsh and competitive Western Conference.

As the 2010-2011 season winded down, the Thunder won 55 games and were the 4th seed in the West with the help of midseason acquisition defensive center Kendrick Perkins, who the Thunder traded for in exchange for Jeff Green. Westbrook was placed on the All-NBA Second Team. His numbers leaped, averaging 21.9 points, 8.2 assists, and 4.6 rebounds per game.

As a testament to his improved shooting and growing maturity, Russell Westbrook improved his field goal percentage to 44%. At that time, he had already established himself as one of the best point guards in the game and one of the best young players in the NBA. Meanwhile, his partner-in-crime won the scoring title for a second straight season.

Other than his much-improved perimeter shooting, Russell Westbrook was finally given free reign as an attacker that season. Everyone knew how relentless of a slasher he was. He always made it a point to get to the basket and go up against the tall trees in the paint. Knowing such, Scott Brooks put all his confidence in Westbrook to try and score the basket when needed. His shot attempts increased by nearly three per game while also improving his field goal shooting. And with an improved number of 7.7 free throws a night, Westbrook was one of the league leaders in drawing fouls because of how he continuously attacked the basket.

However, it was during the 2011 NBA Playoffs that a new concern about Westbrook began to develop. Westbrook's rise had been so sudden and surprising that it seemed to threaten the pecking order of the Thunder. It was clear that despite Westbrook's meteoric rise, Kevin Durant remained the best player on the Thunder. But did Westbrook know that?

Whether or not Westbrook knew whom between KD and himself was the better player is something we cannot answer as Russ was instrumental in OKC's playoff success. In the first round, the Thunder were tasked to go up against the fifth-seeded

Denver Nuggets. Since it was a battle between the two closest seeded teams, it was expected to be a tough series.

The Thunder's dynamic duo immediately showed why they were becoming the best pair of players in the NBA. Westbrook and Durant were seemingly unstoppable in Game 1, combining for 72 of OKC's 107 points to win the game by six points. Russ scored 31 points and had seven assists while KD had 41 points. Both players were efficient from the floor and shot more than 50%. Despite KD being the better player at that time, Russell Westbrook shot one more field goal than Durant. Game 2 was more lopsided, even though the duo did not score as much. In a balanced offensive attack by the Thunder, five players were in the double digits, led by KD and Russ who had 23 and 21, respectively. Again, Russell Westbrook took more shots than Kevin Durant.

When the series shifted over to Denver, another rising Thunder forward stepped up to get the win for OKC. When Durant and Westbrook did not shoot well from the floor as the Nuggets defense swarmed the duo, it was shot blocker Serge Ibaka from the Congo who gave the needed scoring. Ibaka had 22 points, 16 boards, and four blocks. With the Thunder up 3-0 in the series, they were virtually a lock-in for the next round. The Nuggets were able to extend the series to at least one more game by winning a close one in the second game on their home floor.

Back in Oklahoma City for Game 5, Russell Westbrook struggled all night. He could not get a shot to go in, nor could he make plays for his teammates. Moreover, Game 3's hero Serge Ibaka could only score a single point. Once again, it was a one-man show by Kevin Durant who scored 41 points for the second time in the series. With the Thunder winning their first-round encounter, they were on their way to the second round for the first time since relocating to Oklahoma City.

The second round would prove to be more difficult. Their second round opponents were the 8th-seeded Memphis Grizzlies who were fresh out of their first round upset win over the top-seeded San Antonio Spurs. While the Thunder relied on the offensive prowess of Westbrook and Durant, the Grizzlies were primarily a defensive team, and their leading scorer Zach Randolph played out of his mind during the first round.

The Thunder, unfortunately, ceded home court advantage to the Memphis Grizzlies in the opening game of the series. Randolph was still burning hot from his incredible performance against the Spurs. He had 34 points and ten rebounds while their center Marc Gasol had 20 points and 13 boards. The Thunder got outmuscled in the interior even though Westbrook and Durant combined for 62 points. But the Thunder would not allow a second loss on their home floor. They defended Randolph well in Game 2 and allowed him only two made field goals for 15 points. KD and Russ led the game in scoring with 26 and 24 respectively. The big difference was sophomore guard James Harden, who scored 21 off the bench.

The Thunder would lose the series lead once again to the Grizzlies as Memphis won Game 3 back in Tennessee. Even after a solid first half by the OKC Thunder and after leading the game by 13 entering the fourth quarter, the Memphis Grizzlies were able to rally back thanks to their bench performers. Moreover, they were able to limit Russell Westbrook to a poor 7 out of 22 from the field. Though Russ had 23 points and 12 assists to lead the Thunder, he fouled out of the game and the Grizzlies were able to rally back from a big deficit to take the series lead 2-1.

Game 4 would turn out to be an instant classic. The Grizzlies started the game out strong and led by as much as 18 points in the second quarter, intent on taking a 3-1 series lead. The Thunder rallied in the middle of the second quarter to make the game close. They completed their rally in the fourth quarter and managed to send the game into overtime. The Grizzlies' Vasquez knocked down a three-pointer in overtime to send the game into a second extension. In the second overtime, however, Russell Westbrook stepped up and sank a midrange jumper to tie the game for a third overtime. The Grizzlies seemed gassed in the third extension and managed to score only 4 points. Russell Westbrook led the Thunder with 40 big points while KD had 35.

The OKC Thunder would take the series lead for the first time by winning Game 5 on their home floor. It was the complete opposite of their last game as they walloped the Grizzlies with a 27-point victory. The Thunder were so good that neither Russell Westbrook nor Kevin Durant played a lot of minutes. Russ played only 25 minutes and scored only 11 points. KD scored 19 points in 30 minutes. Fighting to keep their season alive, the Grizzlies would tie the series and force a Game 7. They were able to limit Kevin Durant's output with tough, physical defense. KD was limited to 11 points. Meanwhile, Russell Westbrook carried the scoring load for his struggling partner with 27 points in a losing effort.

With a Western Conference Finals berth on the line, the OKC Thunder did not let up a single minute in Game 7. They were able to win every quarter of the match, and they limited the Grizzlies' main players all night long. The OKC duo would have their respective phenomenal games. Kevin Durant scored

39 points on 13 out of 25 shooting. The bigger game came out of Russell Westbrook. Russ only had 12 shots and 14 points. He focused mainly on doing all the other things. Westbrook grabbed ten rebounds and assisted on 14 baskets to record a triple-double. Russell became the first player since Scottie Pippen to record a triple-double in a Game 7. Westbrook's triple double did not come at a more opportune time as he helped his team get to the Western Conference Finals.

Both KD and Russ were merely 22 years old at the time. However, they were already good enough to lead their team to the Conference Finals. Not too many players in the history of the NBA were able to get a chance at an NBA Finals berth at that young of an age. Durant and Westbrook were in a league of their own. However, their roadblock would come in the form of the hungrier Dallas Mavericks led by veterans Dirk Nowitzki, Jason Terry, and Jason Kidd. At that point in the playoffs, Dirk was playing out of his mind and seemed as if he could not miss from the floor.

As soon as the Conference Finals started, Dirk Nowitzki immediately went to business. The big German seemed un-guardable and even uncontainable. He scored against any Thunder player that was put on him, and even got a lot of them in foul trouble. Dirk would score 48 big points for the Mavs.

Meanwhile, Kevin Durant was also in a scoring mood. He had 40 points as Russell Westbrook struggled from the floor to get 20 points. It was a game of free throws. The Thunder had 43 attempts from the line, and the Mavs had 36 with Dirk shooting 24 of them. In the end, the Mavs were too experienced for the young Thunder as they opened the series with a 121-112 victory. Though the Thunder were still unable to defend Dirk Nowitzki in Game 2, they got a lot of help from their bench. James Harden scored 23 points on only nine shots while backup point guard Eric Maynor had 13. Maynor controlled the pace so well that Russell Westbrook only played 28 minutes and had 18 points. KD led the Thunder with 24 points, and the Thunder defeated the Mavs to even up the series at one win apiece.

Sadly, Game 2 was the best the OKC Thunder could muster up in the entire series, even after they were able to force overtime in Game 4. The Dallas Mavericks were too good and experienced, and they won the next three games. Westbrook's best games in the series were Games 3 and 5 where he scored more than 30 in both games. However, he and the Thunder just could not defend Dirk Nowitzki as the Mavs would get the win and the NBA Finals berth. Dallas would eventually win the NBA title that year.

The Thunder lost the series against the Mavs, but it was also an awakening for Russell Westbrook, although such an awakening could not avoid criticism. Over Oklahoma City's playoff run, Westbrook took nearly as many shot attempts as Durant, and in fact, took more shot attempts than Durant in the second round against the Memphis Grizzlies, but Durant scored more points per game than Westbrook in every round.

It was a far different setup in the playoffs than in the regular season. In the 82-game stretch, Kevin Durant shot more than two attempts more than Westbrook did per game. But in the postseason, Russ had 20.2 attempts in that 17-game run while KD barely shot more than him at 20.3 a night. However, Westbrook's efficiency was so low that one would be led to think that he should have given the ball to Durant instead.

Sports analysts wondered what was going through Westbrook's head. Why was he shooting the ball so much instead of giving it to Durant? Westbrook's critics went so far as to suggest that Oklahoma City should trade Westbrook for a pass-first point guard. But the Thunder never paid attention to such an idea. They would build around Westbrook and Durant, confident that the two could lead them to the NBA Finals.

NBA Finals Appearance

An eighth seed in the in the 2009-10 season and a Western Conference Finals appearance during the 2011 playoffs meant that the Oklahoma City Thunder were rising just as fast as their two All-Stars were developing. Kevin Durant's scoring prowess was a given. You could expect him to put up at least 25 points on any given night. But arguably the biggest gear that ran the Thunder engine was Russell Westbrook.

As seen from his first All-Star season, Westbrook ran the OKC Thunder offense and turned it into one of the most potent scoring teams in the league. With his energy and hustle on both ends of the court, Oklahoma City had a player that provided the same kind of effort on offense and defense regardless of whether they were up big or in a huge deficit. While Durant remained to be the leader and best player of the team, the heart and lifeblood of the OKC Thunder was indeed Russell Westbrook.

But questions about the mechanics of the Thunder arose as the lockout-shortened NBA season drew closer. Though the world saw the rise of Russell Westbrook as a star talent in the previous season, they also got to see James Harden's potential when Jeff Green, their former third option, was traded away for a defensive big man. Harden exploded onto the scene late in the season and during the playoffs and was the best player off the bench and a good third option behind KD and Russ.

With James Harden, who was an excellent scorer with the ball in his hands and an even better playmaker than he was given credit for, rising from the ranks as another ball-dominant player, many questioned how the Thunder could operate three ball-handlers at the same time. With Durant and Westbrook, it was as if the two All-Stars were just taking turns scoring. In other instances, Russ was given the green light to make plays for KD. But with Harden developing rapidly, some roles had to be changed, and some possessions had to be decreased to cater to the three talented perimeter players.

It would turn out that in the 2011-12 season, the Thunder were even better than they were in the previous season and proved that their playoff run was more than just a fluke. Though the NBA lockout would shorten training camp, the Thunder did not need a lot of time to get used to each other since the OKC front office kept the core roster intact. Moreover, a lot of Thunder players kept themselves in shape by playing in exhibition games during the lockout.

Showing rust from the long layoff the NBA had and signs that he was not quite acquainted with the new mechanics that the OKC Thunder were playing now that James Harden was given possession of the ball more often, Russell Westbrook struggled at the beginning of the season. In the Thunder's season opener against the Orlando Magic, he would only score 14 points on a mediocre 6 out of 17 shooting from the field. And while he would score 28 points in his second game of the season, the worst game he has played in his entire four-year career came on December 28 at the hands of the Memphis Grizzlies.

Struggling against the defense of Memphis, Russ would only score 4 points while making none of his 13 shot attempts. He was struggling so badly that Brooks opted to play Eric Maynor and James Harden more at the playmaker spot. He could not even impact the game in the other facets and it was evident that he was rusty and out of game shape in that early part of the season. What was worse was that Westbrook was a turnover machine in his first four games. In just a span of four outings, Russ already had a total of 25 turnovers.

Nevertheless, the OKC Thunder were able to get a five-game win streak at the start of the season thanks to the improved play of their core players. While it was Kevin Durant that kept the ship afloat in Westbrook's struggles, it was the development of rising shooting guard James Harden that helped the Thunder make the jump into being one of the strongest contenders for the NBA title, even at that early part of the season. The Thunder were 12-2 in their first 14 games of the season thanks to a collective effort.

Against the same Memphis Grizzlies that forced him to miss all of his 13 shots on December 28, Westbrook finally broke out of his slump by putting up 30 on January 10, 2012. He made 12 of his 20 shots in that game. That win was part of a seven-game winning stretch for the Thunder and the start of Westbrook's personal seven-game streak of scoring at least 20 points. Eight days later, he scored 36 in another good shooting night against the Washington Wizards in a loss.

On January 27, Westbrook finally had double-digit assists for the first time in 19 games as he dished out 11 dimes in a win over the Golden State Warriors. Russ also had 28 points and seven steals in that match. However, it would take long before he would break out of the 10-assist barrier again. The Thunder's reliance on isolation plays and Harden's rise as a playmaker were reasons why Westbrook was not quite the playmaker as he had been in the past two seasons.

While Russell Westbrook's assists numbers were not quite on par with the ones he had been putting up the last two years for the Thunder, his scoring found a way to normalize and even take a slight jump that season. In what was the second outing of an eight-game winning streak, Westbrook exploded for 40 big points against the Denver Nuggets. He made 16 of his 29 attempts in that game. After that, he scored 31 in two consecutive games to help his team make the whole league hear the roar of the Thunder.

The winning formula for the Thunder was easy. While KD, Russ, and Harden took care of the scoring load, Serge Ibaka and Kendrick Perkins handled the defense. Ibaka rose to become the best shot blocker in the NBA in addition to improving his offense. Perkins, though offensively limited, proved to be the missing piece in the Thunder frontline. Many questioned the Thunder when they traded Jeff Green, a rising offensive forward, for a purely defensive center like Perkins. But Kendrick solidified the team's interior defense and provided a lot of toughness and veteran leadership for the Thunder.

With the success that the Thunder saw that season, it was hard not to dismiss the efforts and contributions that Russell Westbrook was providing as a second option for OKC. His best output came on March 23, 2012. In a memorable double-overtime game that saw three players going for at least 40 points in that game, Russell Westbrook was the high man for his team when he broke his career mark and scored 45 points on 17 of 28 shooting from the field to win that entertaining one for the Thunder.

Despite the scoring outbursts from Westbrook, the additional development of Thunder players James Harden and Serge Ibaka meant that Westbrook did not see the ball quite as often as he used to, and his assist totals dropped as Harden's rose. Nevertheless, Westbrook maintained his excellent play and even improved his ever-growing offensive game, averaging 23.6 points and 5.5 assists for the year. His low assist numbers did not mean that he chose to pass less. It only indicated that the Thunder played isolation more often considering they had three players that could create their shots at any point in the game. Kevin Durant also developed into a capable playmaker and his offensive game was also growing.

For the second straight year, Westbrook made the All-Star Team and made an impact in the All-Star Game, where he scored 21 big points. He was also a member of the All-NBA Second Team for the second straight season. He contributed significantly to the success of the OKC Thunder, who won 47 out of 66 games to get the second seed in the West. For the third straight season, Kevin Durant won the scoring title and was a serious contender for the MVP award. Meanwhile, James Harden won the Sixth Man of the Year award in his breakout season as a player. With the trio of superstars leading the

Oklahoma City Thunder, the rest of the NBA was bracing themselves for what the team could do in the playoffs.

In the first round, the Thunder were able to exact their revenge against the Dallas Mavericks. Fresh off their title victory the previous season, the Mavs were still hungry for another one. Unfortunately, they were no longer as strong of a team as they were when they had won the championship. Even though Dirk Nowitzki scored at will, there was nobody to help him as the Thunder utilized each of their stars' offensive capabilities. Russell Westbrook ran roughshod in the first two games by scoring 28.5 points in their Games 1 and 2 victories. Meanwhile, KD top scored with 31 in a win in Game 3. Lastly, the Thunder completed a sweep of the defending champions on the strength of James Harden's 29 points off the bench.

Next, the Thunder had to match up against another Western Conference powerhouse, the Los Angeles Lakers. Though the Lakers seemed to be a team in disarray at the time, they were still very mighty opponents, especially with Kobe Bryant, one of the best players in NBA history, leading them. In addition to Kobe, the Thunder also had to contend with a solid frontline composed of Pau Gasol and Andrew Bynum.

Being the younger and fresher team, the Thunder immediately dominated the Lakers in Game 1 of the series. Though the

Lakers' starting point guard was an athletic player by the name of Ramon Sessions, he still could not contain Russell Westbrook, who minced the Lakers defense on the way to 28 points and nine assists. Game 2 was tighter and much more defense-oriented. With neither team scoring more than 80 points, the Thunder trio was still offensively gifted enough to win the game for Oklahoma 77 to 75.

Kobe Bryant, one of the most talented scorers and most competitive players in the history of the NBA, was not ready to cede the title of the best scorer in the NBA just yet. He scored 36 games in Game 3 as he outscored the three-time reigning scoring champion Kevin Durant, who had 31. Meanwhile, Russ had 21 points in a losing effort. Game 3 was a minor setback, however, as the Thunder would go on to win the next two games. In those two games, the OKC Thunder were able to survive scoring outbursts from Kobe, who had 38 and 42 for Games 4 and 5. Equal to the task was Russell Westbrook. Though Russ was not able to equal the scoring output of the Black Mamba, he would still lead the Thunder in scoring with 37 and 28 in the final two games of the series. The Thunder were off to the Conference Finals for the second straight season. One could argue that the San Antonio Spurs were the best team in the NBA since 1999 because of their consistency in getting into the playoffs year after year. Although the Lakers had won more titles since 1999, the Spurs had had more regular season wins and playoff appearances. In the 2012 playoffs, the Spurs were cruising towards a possible NBA Finals berth as they swept their first two playoff series. Were the Oklahoma City Thunder the third straight team that the Spurs would sweep?

It appeared as such in the first two games of the Western Conference Finals. For the second consecutive season, the Thunder were up against an older and more experienced roster. The Spurs used every ounce of their championship experience to edge out Game 1 on Manu Ginobili's 26 points off the bench as the game became a battle between sixth men. Harden scored 19 off the OKC bench while Russell Westbrook struggled to get his 17. The OKC trio would play a lot better in Game 2 as KD, Russ, and Harden scored 31, 27, and 30 respectively. However, Tony Parker played out of his mind and scored 34 points while Ginobili was still scoring well off the Spurs bench. In the end, the Spurs beat the Thunder in Game 2 120 to 111, and it seemed like OKC was about to become the third team to be swept by the Spurs.

Suddenly, things turned different but better for the Thunder. In some ways, OKC was able to make the series more competitive by winning Game 3 in Oklahoma by 20 big points. It was a balanced effort, and Russ needed only 10 points to help the Thunder to victory. Game 4 was just as surprising as the Thunder created a second quarter cushion big enough to handle a third quarter rally by the Spurs. For the second straight game, Russell Westbrook was severely limited and only scored 7. The Thunder banked on KD, who had 36 big points, and Ibaka, who had a perfect game, going 11 out of 11 from the field and 4 out of 4 on free throws.

The Thunder had done what no other team had in the past two playoff rounds—they beat the Spurs not once, but twice to tie the series. With control over the series on the line, Russell Westbrook suddenly broke out of his scoring slump. He scored 23 points and dished out 12 dimes as the Thunder survived a 34-point outburst by Manu Ginobili.

With an NBA Finals spot on the line, the Spurs played desperately to start the first quarter as they raced on to a 14-point lead that turned to 15 at halftime. It was a tale of two halves. While the Spurs owned the first half, the Thunder dominated the more important second half. Nobody wins in the first half, but the second half is where the game is decided. The Thunder would outscore the Spurs 59 to 36 in the second half by playing tough, physical defense and by shooting the ball a lot better. With Kevin Durant playing every single second of the game, he scored 34 to lead the Thunder while Westbrook, who played 41 minutes, scored 25 on 17 shot attempts. After losing two straight games, the Thunder won four straight to make it to the NBA Finals. It was the first time that the franchise had made it to the NBA Finals since 1996 when they were still the Seattle SuperSonics.

After defeating the Dallas Mavericks, Los Angeles Lakers, and San Antonio Spurs in the 2012 Playoffs, the Thunder had defeated the three best Western Conference teams since 1999. Since that year, that triumvirate of teams had won 10 of the possible 13 NBA championships with five going to the Lakers, 4 to the Spurs, and 1 to the Mavs. By beating those teams, the Thunder ushered in a symbolic "changing of the guard" for the top Western Conference team in years to come.

But they were on their way to facing the team that owned every one of the NBA championship victories since 1999. They were tasked to face the Miami Heat in the NBA Finals in a matchup between Kevin Durant and LeBron James, the two best small forwards in the NBA and possibly even the two best players in the world at that time. It was also a matchup between two teams that had a trio of stars. As we know, the Heat had LeBron James, Dwayne Wade, and Chris Bosh. On the other side, the Thunder had Kevin Durant, Russell Westbrook, and James Harden. More importantly, LeBron and Durant both wanted their first NBA title to solidify their places in NBA history, and Westbrook had to support Durant if the Thunder had any chance of victory.

The Thunder would take Game 1 on the strength of Durant's 36 points and Westbrook's double-double outing with 27 points and 11 assists. It was truly a remarkable coming out party for the Thunder's dynamic duo as they seemed to be a class above the Miami Heat. However, the Miami Heat would bounce back in Game 2 using a strong first quarter. Once again, LeBron led the Heat with 32 points. For the Thunder, KD had another spectacular game with 32 games while Westbrook followed up his double-double performance with a near triple-double game. He had 27 points, eight rebounds, and seven assists, but he only shot 10 out of 26.

On the Heat's home floor, the Thunder found themselves reeling. Though Russ and KD were a phenomenal duo, LeBron and Wade were just as good of a pair, but were more experienced. In Game 3, LBJ and D-Wade combined for 54 points. Meanwhile, the Thunder duo scored only 44 as they struggled to get help from their teammates in a losing effort.

However, Westbrook decided to take it upon himself to lead Oklahoma City. While LeBron guarded Durant, Miami Heat started role player Mario Chalmers at the point guard position and Westbrook saw an opportunity to score. In Game 4, Westbrook erupted for 43 points on 20 for 32 shooting. His 62.5% field goal percentage was the third highest percentage by any player who scored more than 40 points in an NBA Finals game. Russ was making minced meat out of the Heat defense. However, he would also become the bane of his team. Down merely a single possession and with several possessions left on the clock, Westbrook intentionally fouled Mario Chalmers, who sank the two free throws, thinking that they did not have enough time left on the clock for a final attempt. Before that play, Russ also committed a crucial turnover when he dribbled the ball off his leg. And though the Thunder would not have been competitive in that game if it were not for Westbrook's career game, it was ultimately Russ's mistakes that sealed his team's fate.

Aside from that one brilliant game, Westbrook was unable to come through. As had happened in other playoff series, he once again took more shots than Kevin Durant while scoring fewer points, and the Miami Heat defeated the Thunder in 5 games with LeBron James recording a triple-double in the Game 5 clincher. People noticed that Russell Westbrook was taking shots away from the better and much more efficient scorer, Kevin Durant. They would have wanted him to play more of a passing point guard instead of trying to lift his team up by himself despite having several other teammates who could score just as well. But actually, the Oklahoma City Thunder could not have made it all the way to the NBA Finals if it were not for Westbrook's style of play.

Without Harden, Being the Top Seed, and Getting Injured

In addition to the continued concerns about Westbrook trying to do too much, a new problem appeared for the Thunder. Earlier in 2011, Westbrook signed an $80 million extension with the Thunder, but with additional contracts given to Ibaka and Durant, as well as an upcoming deal for Harden, the question now became how Oklahoma City was going to pay for everyone. Unable to do so, the Thunder traded Harden to the Houston Rockets right before the 2012-2013 season began. In exchange for James Harden, they got capable scorer Kevin Martin. While Oklahoma City's record had improved every year since Westbrook had joined the team, it was predicted that they would drop off that year with Harden's departure, especially when Harden immediately showed himself to be a true superstar with the Rockets.

But Russell Westbrook continued to do what he was used to doing since he had broken out of the league to become an All-Star. He was doing everything. Though the Thunder dropped their first game to the San Antonio Spurs where Russ struggled to shoot from the floor, the All-Star point guard pounced on the Portland Trailblazers in their next game on November 2, 2012, to score 32 points on 13 out of 24 shooting from the field.

In the Thunder's fifth game of the season, Westbrook recorded his first double-double of the season against the Chicago Bulls. He had 16 points and 12 assists as he focused on making plays because he struggled against the Chicago defense, going 7 out of 22 from the field. That win was part of a five-game winning streak that gave OKC a 6-2 start through their first eight games. He had three double-doubles in those five wins.

As the season began to unfold, it was becoming ever clearer that the OKC Thunder were nowhere near the predicted drop-off that they were expected to have. In fact, they were even better than advertised and had improved on several of their weaknesses from the previous season. However, the fact of the matter was that the Thunder could only go as far as KD and Russ could take them.

For his part, Russell Westbrook had several memorable performances in the Thunder's 12-game winning streak from

November to December. In just 21 minutes of play, he had 12 points and 11 assists in a huge blowout win against Charlotte. Against Utah for their fourth consecutive win in that streak, he had one of the best stat lines you would ever see from a point guard. With 23 points, 13 rebounds, eight assists, and seven steals, one would say that Russell Westbrook was all over the floor. Russ would have a total of five double-double performances in those 12 straight wins for the Oklahoma City Thunder. They were 21-4 through their first 25 games.

With Westbrook doing his normal damage from every facet of the game, the point guard often flirted with triple-doubles as the season progressed. With James Harden in Houston, Russ had more possessions for himself to either attack the basket or to make plays. That was why his assist numbers were normalizing back to the numbers he had in his first All-Star season.

Moreover, Westbrook had become an even more tenacious rebounder for a player his size. The Thunder did not lack in rebounding, especially with Perkins, Ibaka, and Durant manning the frontline. However, Russell Westbrook helped his big men by chasing after offensive rebounds and loose balls every time he could. The little man would even go up for emphatic rebounds to go coast to coast for transition baskets when defenses were not yet set. He simply knew how to make good use of his energy and nose for the ball.

Although Russell Westbrook was expected to take a momentous leap in scoring as the Thunder was without James Harden, he would remain in control of his scoring opportunities while making sure his teammates were still involved. Westbrook's scoring pace was the same as the previous season, given the fact that Serge Ibaka and Kevin Martin filled in admirably for the scoring hole that Harden left.

Nevertheless, Westbrook still had a lot of excellent moments concerning scoring. From January 14 to 20 of 2013, Russ turned in four straight games of scoring at least 30 points. He first had 36 on the Phoenix Suns followed by 32 and 31-point performances against the Nuggets and the Mavs respectively. That win in Dallas gave his team six consecutive wins before losing to the Denver Nuggets. Russ had 36 points, eight rebounds, and nine assists in that loss.

After seeing another All-Star Game as a participant, Westbrook's production would not decline a bit after being selected for his third midseason classic. He had a then-season high of 37 points together with seven rebounds and nine assists in a win over the Minnesota Timberwolves on February 22. Five days later, he was a model of efficiency when he torched the New Orleans Hornets for 29 points in only 26 minutes as the Thunder won the game by 45. After that match, he went for his season high of 38 points in a narrow loss to the Denver Nuggets. After playing steadily for the Oklahoma City Thunder, who only lost eight games after the All-Star break thanks to their duo of All-Stars, Russell Westbrook finally got his first and only triple-double of the season. He had 23 points, 13 rebounds, and ten assists in a win over the Milwaukee Bucks after several months of consistently flirting with that stat line. He would score at least 30 points on two more occasions before ending the season as one of the top title contenders.

Despite the predictions that the Thunder would see a drop off that season, Westbrook and Durant would have nothing to do with such claims. New Thunder shooting guard Kevin Martin filled in admirably for Harden, and the trio of Ibaka, Westbrook, and Durant now focused on improving the Thunder defense. Oklahoma City jumped from the 11th-best defense in 2011-2012 to the 4th-best defense in 2012-2013, and a lot of that was due to the improved style of the OKC Thunder duo. KD took a page out of LeBron's book after losing to him in the Finals. The transcendent scorer suddenly passed the ball a lot more than he ever had and his assist numbers jumped to almost 5 per game. Meanwhile, Serge Ibaka evolved from being merely a shot blocker to an efficient option on offense as his scoring increased to 13 per game on 57% shooting.

The Thunder improved to win 60 games that season, clinching the best record in the Western Conference for the first time. Westbrook's assist numbers improved with Harden gone, and he averaged 23.2 points, 5.2 boards, and 7.4 assists for the season. He was one of the best rebounding point guards that year and was turning into one of the best all-around players in the whole NBA. It was a testament to the growing game that Russell Westbrook had, and to his desire to do a hundred percent all the time for his team. Once again, he made the All-Star Team and the All-NBA Second Team.

Despite another stellar season for the athletic point guard, detractors could not help but criticize Russell Westbrook all season long for his seemingly selfish and ball-hogging ways. Playing next to Kevin Durant was not a simple task for Russell Westbrook, not because he did not have the right chemistry with the scoring champion, but because he just could not escape getting criticized for looking like he was taking opportunities away from KD.

One might not easily believe it, but Russell Westbrook took more shots than Kevin Durant that season. He attempted nearly 19 shots per game to Durant's 18. However, the differences in their scoring averages were larger than their attempts would like to show. Durant, who averaged 28.1 points, was the better scorer and the more efficient shooter. He shot 51% from the floor, 41.6% from the three-point line, and 90.5% from the foul stripe. Meanwhile, Russ shot average marks of 43.8% from the field and 32.3% from the three-point area.

What do those figures mean for the All-Star duo and Westbrook's critics? It only served their purpose of criticizing Russ all the more. Durant was the league's best scorer and one of the most efficient shooters. Every shot he took was deemed as a "good" shot, whereas every attempt that left Russ' fingertips were seen as "awful" ones considering the notion that point guards were supposed to pass the ball first.[xi]

With that frame of mind and given that Durant was going down the annals of league history as one of its best scorers, the leading thought and criticism about Westbrook were that he should have given the ball more to KD, who was more effective and efficient. Russ was getting lambasted for looking for his shots instead of going down the path of a Rajon Rondo or a Chris Paul, who both wanted nothing more than to involve their teammates more than they wanted to score.

But Russell Westbrook was not that kind of a player. It was not in his DNA to change just because of criticisms. Russ was an attack-first point guard. He was not out there to just make plays for the multiple-time scoring champion. He was on the court to make sure that he put the ball through the hoop at nearly the same rate as his superstar companion. The Thunder would never have wanted him for those qualities. Even Durant acknowledges Westbrook's abilities.

Kevin Durant would openly say that he believed that Russell Westbrook's aggressiveness is what made them an even better team. He accepted that Westbrook, as a point guard, was supposed to have the ball in his hands more and was given more opportunities to score due to the amount of possessions he had. Having no major chemistry issues with Russell Westbrook, Kevin Durant believed that the All-Star point guard was out there to be the team's primary catalyst while he was serving his purpose of being more efficient with his shot selection.[xii] Given the acknowledgment that he had got from his team and his All-Star buddy, Russell Westbrook needed a championship to get the respect he rightfully deserved from the rest of the world.

In the first round of the 2013 Playoffs, the Thunder played against former teammate James Harden's Houston Rockets. But after destroying the Rockets 120-91 in Game 1, disaster struck for Westbrook and the Thunder in Game 2. In the second quarter, Rockets point guard Patrick Beverley went for a steal and collided with Westbrook's knees. Westbrook collapsed to the ground and stood up clutching his knee, hitting the scorer's table in frustration. He would stay in the game and finish with 29 points as the Thunder won Game 2, but a post-game medical examination revealed a meniscus tear in his right knee, a serious injury that can take weeks, if not months, to fully heal.

Westbrook underwent surgery and was ruled out for the remainder of the playoffs. Those who had lambasted Westbrook for taking shots away from Kevin Durant got to watch the Thunder bleed for points to the Rockets. KD and backup point guard Reggie Jackson did just enough to beat James Harden's Rockets. But then they were tasked to face the Memphis Grizzlies in the next round. The Grizzlies dog piled Durant for the rest of the playoffs, something that would have never happened if Westbrook had been there. KD bled every time for his points, and nobody was there to help alleviate the pressure off of him. Even after winning Game 1, KD could not do enough to beat the Rockets, and they were beaten four straight by the Grizzlies who ended what could have been another Finals berth and a possible championship run for the Thunder.

Injury Season, Watching Durant Dominate the League

In his first five seasons in the NBA, Westbrook had not missed a single game, which was one of the longest streaks of continuous play at the time. But as he recovered from his meniscus tear, Westbrook battled continued problems with his knees throughout the 2013-2014 season. He underwent a second knee surgery right before the preseason in October 2013 to repair a loose stitch. People suddenly thought that Westbrook might follow in the steps of Derrick Rose, who never returned to his superstar form after suffering several serious knee injuries. Rose never got his explosiveness back and seemed to be tentative whenever he attacked the basket. Westbrook was always a similar player to Rose, and he could also face the same problems as he tried to come back from his serious injury.

While Westbrook was initially expected to miss the first four to six weeks of the regular season, he only missed the first two games. But Westbrook struggled to recover from the long rehabilitation period. Though he would still score the usual numbers he was putting up, he was far less efficient despite retaining the same tenacity and aggressiveness that had made him a star in the league.

Westbrook never broke out of the 30-point barrier until he scored 31 points together with nine rebounds in a loss to the Golden State Warriors on November 14, 2011. Four days later, he had 30 points, 12 rebounds, and seven assists in a win versus the Denver Nuggets. Against the same Golden State Warriors on November 19, Westbrook had 34 points, seven assists, and five steals. But, though Russ had several great games, they were in between inconsistent and bad performances, which was obviously due to the rust and sluggishness of his recovery period. But even though Westbrook was playing subpar, the OKC Thunder were still winning at a pace deserving of a top playoff seed.

He averaged 21 points over the first two months, his lowest since he first made the All-Star Team. Nevertheless, Russ seemed like he still had his usual explosiveness and attacking mentality. But unlike Rose, Westbrook was just as ferocious on the floor as he was before the injury. He was not afraid of mixing it up at the basket and seemed as if he never lost a step. Though Rose was initially a better player, it was Westbrook's work ethic and ferocity that helped him in his quick return to form after recovering from his injury.

Despite a having some good performances in that early juncture of the season, Russell Westbrook had to sit out for a long time due to the nagging injury. However, he could not rest a few months without putting up one of his signature triple-doubles. He had 14 points, 13 rebounds, and ten assists versus the New York Knicks on Christmas Day when the Thunder won by 29 in Madison Square Garden.

On December 27, 2013, however, Westbrook underwent his third surgery in nine months to reduce swelling in his right knee. Despite playing at a very high level throughout the season, he and the Thunder became cautious, especially because Westbrook always attacked aggressively whenever he played. Having played so few games to begin the season, Westbrook failed to make the All-Star Team for the first time in four years. When Westbrook returned, he continued to rest and miss games here and there throughout the season, and the Thunder were determined to make sure that he would be ready for the playoffs. Down to technically a one-man team, Kevin Durant immediately went to work the moment his partner-in-crime recuperated. KD was simply transcendent and nothing short of amazing during the months of January and February as he went on a scoring spree. In that span, he had 19 straight games with more than 30 points. KD also had a 41-game streak of scoring more than 25 points a night. That streak remains to be the third highest in history, and is the highest since Michael Jordan did it back in his prime. He also scored more than 40 in seven of those games including one 54-point output. Kevin Durant was showing the world what he was capable of without Russell Westbrook. He was quickly becoming the favorite for the coveted Most Valuable Player award. Even when Russ came back in March, KD was still on a tear. He continued his 25-point streak and scored like crazy night after night, including a 51-point night against the Raptors. KD was elevated to the top of the MVP ladder, and he carried the OKC Thunder while Westbrook was not around.

While Westbrook missed many games in 2013-14, he still managed to have an impact in the games he did play. On March 6 against the surprisingly good Phoenix Suns, Westbrook stripped the ball from Suns guard, Goran Dragic, on the very first possession of the game, and finished the season with 36 points, nine assists, and nine rebounds. Five days later, Westbrook played his first game against the Rockets since his injury at the hands of Patrick Beverley. In the highly-anticipated matchup between Westbrook and Beverley, the latter being one of the better defensive point guards in the league, the two quickly got into a scuffle early in the game. Beverly was booed throughout the game for being the reason for the Thunder's early exit the previous season. In the end, Westbrook would get his revenge, scoring 24 points as the Thunder defeated the Rockets 106-98. He finished the season averaging 21.2 points, seven assists, and a career high of 5.7 rebounds, an incredible number for a point guard. Healthy at last by the end of the season, the Thunder geared up for a 2014 playoffs run, seeking to gain their first title.

As the playoffs began, the second-seeded Thunder faced a very familiar foe in the first round: The Memphis Grizzlies. But this time around, it would be an entirely different series with Russell Westbrook healthy and ready to avenge the last season's defeat. Aside from having a healthy Russ, the team was also banking on the remarkable season KD was having.

Russell Westbrook would storm out of the gates and come out firing for the Thunder. Westbrook pushed the pace hard and drained one jump shot after another, scoring a total of 12 points in the opening quarter of Game 1. It was contagious, and Kevin Durant also caught fire early in the game as the Thunder's dynamic duo combined for 35 points in the first half and built an enormous half-time lead over the Grizzlies. However, after the Thunder led by 25 points, the Grizzlies made a fierce rally that cut the deficit to just four points at the end of three quarters. But Oklahoma City would hold on to a 100-86 series opener win with Durant top-scoring with 33 points and Russell

Westbrook adding 23 points, five assists, and a team high of 10 rebounds.

It was obvious that the Thunder were a different team with Westbrook back because while they were facing virtually the same team that eliminated them in the 2013 playoffs, the Thunder had a smooth sailing outing with both Durant and Westbrook on the front end leading their charge. The world saw a glimpse of what the Oklahoma City Thunder were capable of with both of their superstars healthy and playing beyond their capabilities.

The Grizzlies would roar back in Game 2 and tie the series at one game apiece after a heart pounding 111-105 overtime thriller. Once again, the Thunders' superstars put up big numbers with Durant scoring 36 points including 20 after the third quarter, and Westbrook added 29 big points. But the duo only combined for 23-56 shooting and the team shot under 40% as the Grizzlies stole the Thunder's home court advantage away. Game 3 was played in a different venue, but it had the same results: The Grizzlies beat the Thunder for the second straight game in overtime, 98-95. Durant and Westbrook would score 30 points apiece, but once again, the two shot poorly and combined for a paltry 19-53 from the field.

Facing a possible 3-1 hole, the Thunder would salvage Game 4 92-89 in another overtime game, despite Westbrook and Durant struggling for the third straight game. The All-Star pair had 15 points each, but were an aggregate 11-45 from the field. This time, reserve guard Reggie Jackson came off the bench to score 32 points to lead OKC back in the series.

The teams would alternate wins in the next two games with the Grizzlies taking Game 5 and the Thunder coming back strong in Game 6 after the "Mr. Unreliable" issue with Kevin Durant. With the series tied at 3-3, the stage was set for what was going to be the Thunder's defining moment.

The Thunder had not been ousted in the first round of the playoffs since 2010 but were facing possible elimination against last season's conquerors, the Memphis Grizzlies. However, the young Thunder tandem played their best in the game they needed most.

Kevin Durant scored 33 points and went 12-18 from the field and 5-5 from three-point distance in Game 7. However, it was Russell Westbrook's all-around brilliance that sealed the series, clinching a 120-109 win in Game 7. Westbrook scored 27 points, grabbed ten rebounds, and dished off 16 assists in his second triple-double in three games. It was also Russ's second career Game 7 triple-double. Westbrook shot 10-16 from the field including 2-2 from three-point distance and 5-6 from the foul line. Westbrook's 16 assists tied the franchise record for most assists in a playoff game set by Nate McMillan in 1987, when the team was still in Seattle.

In the second round, the Thunder would face the Los Angeles Clippers. After the Clippers had stolen Game 1 in Oklahoma City 122-105, the Thunder responded with a 112-101 win in Game 2 behind another herculean effort by Russell Westbrook. The feisty UCLA product scored 31 points on top of 10 rebounds and ten assists to lead the Thunder. He would score 23 points and hand out 13 assists in a Game 3 win at the Staples Center. Westbrook then exploded with 38 points, 11-23 field goal shooting, and 14-16 from the free throw line in Game 5, as the Thunder put the troubled Clippers on the brink of elimination. With the Clippers playing amidst the distraction of a racism allegation hurled against their owner Donald Sterling, the Oklahoma City Thunder advanced to their third Conference Finals appearance in four years with a 104-98 win in Game 6. Westbrook had another exceptional quarterbacking job with 12 assists and 19 points.

However, the Thunder would suffer yet another big blow to their championship aspirations after center Serge Ibaka suffered a calf injury in their series clincher against the Clippers. Their worst fears were confirmed one day after their Game 6 win as Ibaka was declared out for the remainder of the playoffs.

Without their defensive anchor, the Thunder struggled in Games 1 & 2, losing both games by a combined margin of 52 points. Westbrook also struggled in the first two games, averaging 20 points with just five assists. But it was the absence of Serge Ibaka that doomed the Thunder as they gave up an average of 117 points per game in the first two games of the series.

The theory of Ibaka's presence was proved in Game 3 when the Congo-born big man returned to the Thunder as the series shifted back to OKC. Ibaka scored 15 points, grabbed seven rebounds, and blocked four shots, and the Thunder kept their season alive with a 106-97 win. Russell Westbrook led the Thunder with 26 points, eight rebounds, seven assists, and three steals. Westbrook would play at a higher level in Game 4 as he became the only player in NBA history other than Michael Jordan to post 40 points, five rebounds, ten assists, and five steals in a single playoff game. With Westbrook's incredible stat line, the Thunder beat the Spurs for the second straight game and tied the series at two games apiece. However, the Spurs would kick into higher gear and beat the Thunder in the next two games to advance to the NBA Finals for the second consecutive season.

Despite another strong regular season, the Thunder failed to win an NBA title after another critical injury hurt their playoff run. In 2013, it was Russell Westbrook, and in 2014, it was Serge Ibaka. It was frustrating for Westbrook, who had started to develop into an all-around monster on the court, and was particularly frustrating for Kevin Durant, who was named the NBA's 2014 MVP after a sensational scoring season. KD would put the growing controversy between him and Russ to rest, saying in his MVP acceptance speech that Westbrook did not need to change who he was despite the criticisms he had faced.

The narratives for that long injury-riddled season for Russell Westbrook were simple ones. Without Russ, Kevin Durant could lead the Oklahoma City Thunder by his lonesome towards a strong season finish. Without Russ, KD could put up MVP numbers and look like the best player in the NBA on any given night. Without Russ in the regular season, the Thunder were fine as long as the rest of the team remained healthy.

However, Russell Westbrook's value became more evident in the playoffs. Kevin Durant could not carry the Thunder on his own in the playoffs without the help of the team's catalyst, Russell Westbrook, no matter how transcendentally good he was during the regular season in his quest towards winning the Most Valuable Player award. Westbrook's fire and passion for the game of basketball fueled the Thunder's deep postseason run as he consistently dominated the game in every other facet that Durant could not whether it was in hustle, energy, playmaking, tenacity, or aggressiveness. As much as Durant was an MVP on his own, he needed Russell Westbrook to do the things he could not.

Though their season ended without a chance at the NBA title, nobody could blame them for losing to the San Antonio Spurs. As good as KD and Russell Westbrook were in the playoffs, the Spurs were on a level far above everyone else in the NBA. The Thunder were just not as experienced or well-coached as the Spurs were that year. But little did they know that the frustrations and trials that they experienced were only a prelude of things to come.

Russell Westbrook's One-Man Show

In October 2014, the Thunder announced that 2014 MVP Kevin Durant had suffered a Jones Fracture, a broken bone at the base of his little toe. He was diagnosed to miss the first 6-8 weeks of the 2015 regular season, and that meant that the Thunder would have to rely heavily on Russell Westbrook to start the 2015 season. Bad news was also quick to strike as Russell Westbrook would miss 14 games at the onset of the season due to an injury he suffered in their season opener.

Before the announcement of the injury, the Thunder were already planning to limit Durant's minutes in the 2015 NBA season after their star forward opted out of playing for Team USA in the 2014 FIBA Basketball World Cup, citing that he needed physical and mental rest. Durant played the most minutes of any NBA player since 2007 at 20,717 minutes, and the wear and tear were starting to take their toll on the newly crowned MVP. Since Durant had only missed 32 games in his first seven seasons in the NBA, this would be the first time that the Thunder would be playing without their MVP for a prolonged period. Apparently, there were unchartered waters ahead for the Thunder.

While Durant had carried the Thunder in the previous season for 36 games without their starting point guard, Westbrook had only played five games without Durant in the last five seasons. One of those games was a regular season finale where Durant was forced to sit out while Westbrook played token minutes to keep a consecutive games-played streak going. The other four were during the 2010-2011 season when OKC went 3-1 where Westbrook averaged 26.7 points and 7.0 assists per game.

There were more reasons to be statistically optimistic, though. During the 2012-2013 season, the Thunder were +9.5 points per 100 possessions when Durant was off the court. Then in the

2014 season, Russell Westbrook played a total of 1,411 minutes. Of those, only 41 minutes were played without Kevin Durant. Westbrook scored a total of 46 points in 35 field goal attempts over that period. Still, the sample size of the Thunder's success without Durant was too few for the number of games Durant was expected to miss. But one thing was sure: the Thunder would have to lean on Westbrook like they had never had to before.

While Durant's absence was an opportunity for Westbrook to come out of his partner's shadows, he did not want all the attention for himself. Two weeks before the season started, Westbrook talked to Royce Young of ESPN and said that it was not about him, it was about their team. Westbrook said he could not win games all by himself and that he wanted to take the attention off of himself and put it on the Thunder as a team because winning was about the Thunder and what they could do as a team.

Westbrook had a point. The Thunder had a healthy Serge Ibaka, and together with Westbrook, they had two All-Star caliber players and a worthy supporting cast led by Reggie Jackson, Dion Waiters, Steven Adams, and newcomer Anthony Morrow. This was a team that held court without Westbrook for nearly half of the last season and finished the previous season with 59 wins. The Thunder was going to miss Durant very much, and they would not be title contenders without him, but with the line-up they had, they were still a very solid team capable of holding their ground until Durant returned.

The OKC Thunder opened the 2015 NBA regular season on October 29, 2014, against the Portland Trail Blazers at the Moda Center in Portland, and by that time, it was not only Kevin Durant who was injured. Reggie Jackson, Jeremy Lamb, Anthony Morrow, Grant Jerrett, and Mitch McGary were all out because of minor injuries. With a depleted lineup, there was clearly too much pressure on Russell Westbrook's shoulders. But Westbrook was ready for his coming out party.

The Thunder led for most of the game with Westbrook scoring 26 points in the first half, but the Blazers caught up with a visibly tired Thunder squad and outscored them 31-12 in the final quarter to win 106-89. Westbrook finished with 38 points and six assists, but he shot just 11-26 from the field. The only other two players that scored in the double digits along with Westbrook were Serge Ibaka (10 points) and undrafted third-year man Lance Thomas (14 points), while all five Portland Trail Blazers starters scored at least 10 points. The difference in the production of the starting lineups clearly showed that the Thunder were missing a lot of players, and whether they liked it or not, it was going to be a problem that they would have to play with in the coming weeks.

It was not much that the Thunder lost on opening night because they were on the road and it was just one game in an 82-game schedule. But the difference in manpower was evident. The Thunder got the game they needed from Westbrook, but the team needed more healthy bodies to help him win games and keep the team afloat while waiting for Durant to return.

On October 30, 2014, The Thunder traveled to the Staples Center to face the L.A. Clippers in their second game of the season and their second consecutive game on the road. But instead of rebounding from the opening night loss to the Blazers, the Thunder lost to 93-90 and suffered yet another major setback.

Russell Westbrook exited the game at the 6:35 mark of the second quarter after injuring his hand while going up for a rebound and hitting teammate Kendrick Perkin's elbow. Westbrook was seen grimacing in pain as he tried to clench his fist while heading to the locker room. He would return to the Thunder bench in the third quarter with a bag of ice wrapped around his right hand. Westbrook did not play again, though, and he left for the dugout for good before the start of the final period. Westbrook even had to be restrained from a heckling fan on the way out as frustration began to set in.

The Thunder's worst fears became a reality when post-game X-ray results revealed that Westbrook had suffered a minor fracture of the second metacarpal of his right hand. Westbrook underwent surgery on his right hand on November 1, 2014, and was declared out of action for at least four weeks. Now the Thunder were without both Durant and Westbrook. They were without a superstar and needed to rely on developing point guard Reggie Jackson.

Seven games later, the Thunder were 3-6 on the season and had an entirely different look. Reserve guard Reggie Jackson was the team's leading man and led the team in scoring at 20 points per game and in assists at 8.3 per game. The once high-scoring Thunder team was averaging just 92 points per game and were far from the perennial title contenders that they had been in the last four seasons. The losing did not end there.

Six straight losses dropped the Thunder to the bottom of the Western Conference with a 3-12 record, and the worries had now turned to doubts about whether the Thunder could still recover from the slow start and make the playoffs in a very deep Western Conference. But with Durant and Westbrook's recovery timetable right on schedule, Coach Scott Brooks was still positive that his team would be able to make a 360-degree turnaround once his stars returned to action.

Westbrook returned to action on November 28, 2014, against the New York Knicks. Russell Westbrook picked up where he had left off, scoring 32 points along with seven rebounds and eight assists, and led the Thunder to a rousing 105-78 win over the New York Knicks for their second consecutive win and first back to back wins of the season. But these were the Knicks who, like the Thunder, were a weak 4-12 before the game. One game after Westbrook's season debut, Kevin Durant returned to action for the Thunder after missing the first seventeen games of the season.

The Thunder lost in Durant's season debut, but seeing their dynamic duo together for the first time that season was a sigh of relief for the Thunder faithful. But then again, this was still not where they envisioned they would be when their superstars returned. OKC had hoped for a split of their games during the absence of their stars. Instead, they were 5-13 after the first game with Durant and Westbrook playing together. The Thunder were 10.5 games off the Western Conference top seed and five games behind the 8th place Phoenix Suns.

After losing their first game with Durant and Westbrook together, the Thunder won eight of their next nine games to pull themselves to within half a game of 8th-seeded Phoenix in the race for the final playoff spot in the Western Conference. Their superstar combo was clicking again, but this time around, it looked as if the roles were reversed and that there was a new MVP in Oklahoma City. With Kevin Durant not yet back to his full MVP state, Russell Westbrook was the one carrying the load.

Russell Westbrook was the architect of OKC's 8-2 winning run. He averaged 28.2 points, 7.6 rebounds, 7.7 assists, and 1.7 steals per game during those ten games. Westbrook's win-share per 48 minutes total at that time was .296, which was second best in the entire NBA, which proved that he was producing the wins individually. Russ had several memorable games while putting up insane numbers night in and night out.

In the Thunder's seven-game winning streak in December, Russ scored below 25 points only once while making sure he was up to the challenge of filling in for his four-time scoring champ companion. He would then score at least 30 points three consecutive times before exploding for 40 markers and ten rebounds in a narrow loss to the Trailblazers before Christmas Day. On Christmas, he had 34 points, 11 assists, and five steals in a win against the San Antonio Spurs.

Though Russ was on the rise at that juncture of the season, the Thunder were still far from their championship-contending form as Kevin Durant's numbers were not as good as the previous year when he won MVP honors. In fact, Durant was averaging 8 points fewer in their wins than in their losses. Sure, the Thunder were playing Durant 10 fewer minutes per game than his career average, but that was because they wanted to break him in slowly after foot surgery. Still, Westbrook's rise as the Thunder's leading man was meteoric, and he was coming into his own as a full-fledged superstar who was no longer just a sidekick.

On January 16, 2015, Westbrook became the fifth player in NBA history to rack up a stat line of 15-15-15 with 17 points, 15 rebounds, and a career-high of 17 assists during a big 127-115 win over the league-leading Golden State Warriors. But that was not the end of Russell Westbrook's mission of putting up crazy numbers every night. He would have 40 points in a sorry loss to the New York Knicks on January 28 before mixing it up with the Orlando Magic for his second triple-double of the season five days later. In that win, he had 25 points, 11 rebounds, and 14 assists.

The scoring barrages kept coming for Russell Westbrook, who was simply on a tear and looking like he was on a mission towards the next level of his greatness. On February 4, 2015, Westbrook tied his career-high of 45 points in a 102-91 win over the New Orleans Pelicans. He hit 18 of his 31 attempts that game. Two days later against the same team, Westbrook recorded a new career high with 48 points. Impressively, Westbrook, on his way to recording 48 markers, was still playing his usual all-around brand. He nearly had a triple-double after compiling nine rebounds and 11 assists in that narrow loss.

While Westbrook's stock continued to rise, Kevin Durant was in and out of the lineup after his December 2 return. Durant injured his ankle in their December 18 game against the Golden State Warriors and returned again on December 31, 2014. He also sprained his left big toe in January 2015. The series of injuries to Durant stalled OKC's plans of taking over the 8th playoff spot. Entering the All-Star break, the Thunder were still a half-game behind the Phoenix Suns for the final playoff spot in the Western Conference

The 2015 NBA All-Star Game was the crowning glory of Russell Westbrook's spectacular season. As he was starting to hear the MVP chants in Oklahoma City, Westbrook turned in a performance for the ages at the world's grandest stage, Madison Square Garden, to lead the Western Conference All-Stars to a

163-58 win over the East. Westbrook was not a starter, but once his number got called, he wasted no time re-introducing himself to his peers and the fans. Westbrook drained his first four baskets and hit three consecutive three-point baskets to start the second quarter. At the half and after an assortment of highlight-reel dunks and daredevil drives, Westbrook had compiled an All-Star game record of 27 first half points.

Westbrook slowed down a bit in the second half, needing 13 more shot attempts to score his final 14 points. His biggest basket of the game came at the 2:21 mark of the final period when he drained a three-pointer that gave the West a commanding 158-149 lead. Then, with one second left in the game, Westbrook was at the foul line to shoot one more free throw. He was at 40 points, two points short of Wilt Chamberlain's 53-year-old All-Star game record of 42 points. But Westbrook knocked down the free throw to seal the win and end the game with 41 points, just one point shy of the record. After the game, Westbrook admitted he was going for Wilt's mark, saying he even tried to miss the second free throw.

Westbrook shot 16-28 from the floor and 5-9 from three-point distance. But he made the most of his playing time and became the third player after Chamberlain and Michael Jordan to score at least 40 points in an All-Star Game. Wilt Chamberlain scored his 42 points in 37 minutes, and Westbrook was one point shy in just 25 minutes and 33 seconds of floor time. That is what made it more impressive, and also why he was named All-Star Game MVP. After the game, Westbrook said, "It's definitely a blessing, man. You never want to take no games off, especially an All-Star Game to get a chance to go out and show your talents. I'm blessed to be able to play the game that I love, and definitely happy we got the win."

Westbrook played like Russell Westbrook -- super-charged and feisty. He left no stone unturned, held no prisoners, and played like a man on a mission. This was the All-Star game where the players were supposed to have fun and enjoy the weekend, but for Westbrook and his Thunder, there was no time to take games off because they had a playoff bus to catch and had to play each game like their season depended on it. Westbrook's All-Star Game MVP performance was a much-needed confidence booster for the Thunder, which had been through a lot of struggles during the season.

Knowing they needed one big push during the second half of the season, the Thunder traded Reggie Jackson to the Detroit Pistons and Kendrick Perkins to the Utah Jazz at the trade deadline and acquired Enes Kanter, D.J. Augustin, Kyle Singler, and Steve Novak from those two teams. Jackson was having a career season, but the backup guard was headed for free agency. On the other hand, Perkins became dispensable with Kanter on board, and his salary was used to complete the three-team deal.

The trade deadline move was not a game-changer for the Thunder, but the team acquired valuable assets who would be able to help Durant and Westbrook on their final drive to the post-season. However, bad news came again when Kevin Durant was forced out of the lineup on February 22 to undergo a pain-reducing procedure on his surgically-repaired right foot. Westbrook was on his own again, and with their season on the line, he upped his game a couple of gears higher. Just right after the All-Star break, he had seven consecutive double-doubles, which included five of the most statistically crazy games you will ever see in the NBA, let alone a point guard at that.

In their first game, again without Durant, Westbrook tied his career high of 17 assists in a 119-94 romp over the Denver Nuggets. Two days later, he posted his third triple-double of the season despite sitting out the entire fourth quarter of their 105-92 win over the Indiana Pacers. This was only the beginning of what was going to be a long rampage for Russell Westbrook. He would then score 39 big points while also rebounding 14 misses and assisting on 11 field goals.

Two games later, Westbrook became the first person since LeBron James in 2009 to record three consecutive triple-doubles. Despite the loss to the Portland Trailblazers in that match, Russ had 40 points, 13 rebounds, and 11 assists. You rarely see players scoring huge numbers while also recording double digit assists and rebounds. He finished the month of February with averages of 31.2 points, 9.1 rebounds, and 10.3 assists per game to become the 2nd player in NBA history to average 30-9-10 in a calendar month with at least ten games played. The only other player to achieve that was Oscar Robertson, who did it multiple times.

But before the month was over, Westbrook broke the zygomatic arch bone in his cheek during a February 27 loss to the Blazers. After missing the next game after having corrective surgery on his cheek, Westbrook returned to basketball action wearing a mask to protect his injury. The facemask would become symbolic as the masked Westbrook would go on an incredible statistical rampage in the coming games to push the Thunder to the playoffs. Russell Westbrook was slowly becoming "Beastbrook."

In their next game on March 4, Westbrook recorded a fourth consecutive triple-double by setting a career-high 49 points together with 16 rebounds and ten assists. In doing so, he was also the first player since Michael Jordan in 1989 to put up four straight triple-doubles. He also became the first player since Jordan to have back-to-back triple-doubles with at least 40 points. Also, his 49-point output was the highest scoring total in a triple-double game since Larry Bird scored 49 in 1992. Bird was a 6'9" forward while Russ was barely 6'3" and playing at the backcourt. However, Westbrook's historic run ended in their next game on the following night when he was held to 43 points, eight rebounds, and seven assists in a 105-108 losing effort to the Chicago Bulls.

Three days later, however, Westbrook resumed his triple-double exploits and added another two more triple-doubles in the next three games to level up his season total to seven and improve his streak to six-in-eight games. He had 30 points, 11 rebounds, and a career high of 17 assists in a win against the Toronto Raptors right after he scored 43 in a losing effort to the Bulls. The beastly Russell Westbrook then had 29 points, ten rebounds, and 12 assists in a win over the Timberwolves on March 13.

While Russell Westbrook could be charged and criticized for simply padding up his stats at that point of the season, the argument against it was that he simply had to do everything on the floor given the fact that it was his style of play. Nobody was out there to help him lead the OKC Thunder to a possible playoff push. The Thunder, thanks to the historic efforts of their point guard, won 13 of their last 18 games after the All-Star break to pull closer to the playoff race. Russ would have his 9th triple-double of the season on March 20 before helping his team win their 13th game in 18 tries.

On another note, the offense was running smoothly despite Westbrook's astronomical numbers. While he was scoring big numbers, he was also making sure that he got his teammates involved. The only other sources of offense on the team were Dion Waiters and Enes Kanter. However, Westbrook's rising talent in playmaking had everyone looking like All-Star scorers out on the floor. More importantly, the Thunder had grabbed the 8th spot in the West and were just four games behind Dallas for the 7th spot despite all of the adversities they had gone through. However, their troubles refused to end.

On March 27, Durant was finally shut down by the team for the remainder of the season to undergo yet another foot surgery. This was perhaps the biggest setback of the season because the Thunder were hoping that a healthy Durant would combine with the rampaging Westbrook in the final month of the regular season and take them deep into the playoffs. But that was not meant to be.

Westbrook would get two more triple-doubles to finish the regular season with 11 triple-doubles and become the 7th player to record at least ten triple-doubles in a single season since 1986. He had 31 points, 11 rebounds, and 11 assists in a loss to the Dallas Mavericks. That loss was the start of their skid as the season was winding down. Russ would then have 40 points, 11 rebounds, and 13 assists in yet another loss, which was the third of four straight.

But the Thunder would finish the season with a dismal 5-7 record and miss the playoffs for the first time in six years, and for only the second time since moving to Oklahoma City. Westbrook would finish the season in a blaze of glory by scoring 37 points, grabbing eight rebounds, and handing off seven assists in a 138-113 win over the Minnesota Timberwolves.

The Thunder finished the regular season tied with the New Orleans Pelicans at 45-37 with the Pelicans having to beat the San Antonio Spurs and snap the champs' 11-game winning streak to get there. The Pelicans earned the playoff nod because they owned the tiebreaker against the Thunder by beating them thrice during the regular season, including one game that was decided by a buzzer-beating three-pointer by Anthony Davis.

Westbrook was a serious contender for the MVP award for his magnificent one-man show throughout the season in trying to get the Thunder into the playoffs. He finished fourth in the MVP voting behind eventual winner Stephen Curry and runners-up James Harden, his former teammate, and perennial MVP contender LeBron James. Had the Thunder made it to the playoffs that season, Russ would have finished higher in the MVP voting and could have won the award. He finished the 2014-15 NBA season with career highs in every facet of his game. He averaged 28.1 points, 7.3 rebounds, 8.6 assists, and 2.1 steals per game. Westbrook was the league's best scorer that season by barely edging out James Harden. He had 11 triple-doubles for the whole season and was nominated to the All-NBA Second Team for the fourth time in his career.

While the world got to see what KD was capable of without Russ in 2014, Westbrook made the world realize how much of a transcendent talent he was in 2015 without Durant. The 2014-15 season proved that Westbrook was not merely a sidekick that was feeding off the attention and the greatness of a four-time scoring champion and MVP. He was not merely a selfish player going out on the floor just to pad stats and call his number. Russell Westbrook was more than that as he gave his all just to push his team into the playoff picture.

Had Russell Westbrook been healthy the whole season and had Durant decided to sit out the rest of the way earlier than expected, the Oklahoma City Thunder would have fared better relying solely on Russ instead of trying to squeeze out production from a hobbled KD. The Thunder, even without Durant, were still certainly playoff contenders simply because they had one of the most transcendent all-around players the league has ever seen. Westbrook's passion, intensity, emotion, and dedication to the game of basketball got him the adoration of the world that season.

Nobody could ever argue that the 2014-15 season was Russell Westbrook's coming out party as a member of the most elite players in the league. Joining the likes of LeBron James, Kevin Durant, and Stephen Curry in that club, Westbrook had reached a level far above the rest of the league and far beyond what he was used to be capable of. However, there was a question of whether Russ had already peaked.

As Oklahoma City Thunder general manager Sam Presti would say, Westbrook had already reached a level where one could barely improve already.[xiii] Russ was already making vast strides that he probably could not stretch his legs out more for the widest strides possible. He was at the top of his game and was nowhere near going down. But could Westbrook even make a higher leap than he already did in the past season?

Sam Presti thoroughly believed that his superstar point guard could still improve on the already historic and beastly season that Russ put up. Presti would say that what could still make Russell Westbrook a better player were small and incremental improvements to what was already one of the most all-around and balanced game in league history.

For all of his abilities in scoring and in making plays for others, Russell Westbrook was still finding a balance between his penchant for putting up all-around numbers and his competitive mentality that demanded him to win all the games they possibly could. There were times when he was so focused on his hot hand in scoring that he would forget to make the proper plays for his teammates. And there were also moments when Russ was so caught up in chasing triple-doubles by grabbing rebounds and in setting his teammates up that he would forget that what was needed for the team to win was for him to score.[xiii]

While Russell Westbrook had an amount of talent that seemed endless, there were also questions about whether or not he could still be the same best in the next season given the fact that there were several changes. First off, Scott Brooks, who was the only coach he has truly had since coming over to the NBA, was the one who instilled a lot of confidence and trust in Russ. Westbrook might not have the same faith and role under new head coach Billy Donovan, who was a college coaching legend in Florida. Westbrook might not thrive in a new system or might not even be comfortable with a new coach for all the world knows.

While it cannot be considered a significant change, the return of a fully healthy Kevin Durant might hurt the pecking order of the Oklahoma City Thunder after Russell Westbrook had fully established himself as a man capable of leading a team on his own. After seeing Westbrook winning the scoring championship the previous season and making historic stat lines across the board, one might question whether Russ would still be the same beast with KD back to full health. Nevertheless, Russell Westbrook's focus was always about winning. He would do nothing less than sacrificing his numbers if it meant a title for his team.

The New Mr. Triple-Double, Coming Up Short, Final Season With KD

Coming into the new season, everybody expected the OKC Thunder to compete for the title again. KD was coming back healthy while Russ was just coming off an amazingly historic NBA season for himself. The Thunder were also delighted about the news that Donovan had been working well with Westbrook over the offseason. The former Florida head coach was so impressed with the superstar point guard's abilities that he would often seem like a father proud of his son's accomplishments.[xiii]

Often having gone through isolations plays and take-your-turn moments with Kevin Durant under the coaching of Scott Brooks, Russell Westbrook was going to be a real point guard as indicated by how Donovan was often tutoring Russ on how to communicate with his teammates and become a better floor leader.[xiii] Great point guards like Jason Kidd, Steve Nash, and Chris Paul were often good communicators, which only served them better when it came to finding open teammates as the playmaker begins to understand his teammates' tendencies and intentions on the floor. That was going to be the next step in Westbrook's continuing evolution coming into the new season.

Because of a healthier and more complete team coupled with the positivity and optimism of what Billy Donovan's system did to Russ and KD, the OKC Thunder were obviously going to be one of the best teams in the West. This was especially because their dynamic duo had already felt like how it was to lead a team by their respective lonesome and how difficult it was to try and win a title without each other's help.

Still waiting for the return of KD, Westbrook started where he had left off a season ago. He would lead the Thunder to three straight victories at the outset of the season. With him having a performance of 33 points and ten rebounds in the first game while also putting up 48 points, 11 rebounds, and eight assists in the second game for OKC, it was clear that Beastbrook rampage was not a fluke in the last season.

Though Durant would miss a few games in the first few weeks of the season, the Oklahoma City Thunder still regained the full strength of their lineup in the 2015-16 season. They became an even better offensive threat, especially because of newly extended big man Enes Kanter and reliable shooting guard Dion Waiters coming off the bench. Serge Ibaka also evolved into a capable outside shooter while Steven Adams developed into a good starting center.

While people initially thought that the Thunder offense would both start and end with Russ and KD, they were wrong. The Thunder's dynamic duo still scored a lot of points for the team, but made it a point to involve the whole team. You would rarely see the two try to take over games by themselves. They would only do so whenever the rest of the team failed to contribute.

KD has been having a good assist season with more than 4 per game. But what was surprising was how Russell Westbrook evolved into a "true point guard" seven seasons after NBA scouts said he could not become one.

Westbrook would start the season with at least eight assists in his first nine games. He had double-digit dimes in seven of those nine outings that saw two triple-double efforts. Not intent on ceding his crown as the top triple-double master in the NBA, Russ had 22 points, 11 rebounds, and 11 assists on November 10, 2015, in only 28 minutes of action. He then put up 21 points, 17 rebounds, and 11 assists three days later in a win over the Philadelphia 76ers.

Proving he never lost his place as the reigning NBA scoring champion, Westbrook scored 40 points together with 14 assists in a loss to the Memphis Grizzlies on November 16. Two nights later, he had 43 points on 14 out of 25 shooting from the floor and 15 out of 20 shooting from the stripe in a win over the Pelicans. He did all that while shooting efficient numbers from anywhere on the floor.

As Kevin Durant was steadily returning to the form that made him an NBA MVP, Russell Westbrook dialed the shooting down to focus on the other aspects that he excelled at—everything else. Russ would run a team like a true point guard would do as he shot fewer attempts and began passing and looking for his teammates. For a while, Russell Westbrook was even leading the league in assists before he was overtaken by Rajon Rondo and Chris Paul in that category. Nevertheless, this was a player that was never regarded as a true point guard and one that was always criticized for his seemingly selfish attack-first mentality.

Westbrook had his third triple-double of the season on December 6 by posting 19 points, 11 rebounds, and ten assists while only attempting 13 shots. And in 25 minutes of play in a blowout win over the Grizzlies, he had 13 points and 16 assists. With him leading the point while Durant did his damage by draining buckets, the OKC Thunder were back to their championship-contending form as they were merely behind the Golden State Warriors and the San Antonio Spurs, who were both experiencing historic seasons, all season long.

Westbrook would then have back-to-back triple-doubles in the middle of January in blowout wins against the Timberwolves and the Heat respectively. He had 12 points, 11 rebounds, and ten assists versus Minnesota before going for 13 points, ten rebounds, and 15 dimes on Miami. With those triple-doubles and the few amount of shots he was taking, Russ seemed like an incarnation of Jason Kidd out there. Westbrook would finish a six-game winning streak with 15 dimes on the Charlotte Hornets.

The triple-doubles kept coming for the new Mr. Triple-Double of the NBA as the All-Star Weekend was fast approaching. After posting back-to-back all-around triple-double efforts at the end of January 2016, Westbrook had 24 points, 14 assists, and a career-best 19 rebounds in a win over the Orlando Magic for his third consecutive triple-double. That effort wrapped up Russ' first half of the season as he was on his way to an All-Star start in Toronto.

Unlike the previous season when he won the MVP of the midseason classic, Russell Westbrook was an All-Star starter for the first time in his NBA career arguably because of the monstrous numbers he was putting up on a daily basis for the Oklahoma City Thunder. And despite the fact that all the focus was on the retiring Kobe Bryant, who was playing his 18th and final All-Star Game, Westbrook put on another show for the fans in Toronto.

Playing 22 minutes all game long, Russ kept the motor running for the Western Conference All-Stars, who dominated their Eastern Conference counterparts in the second half of the match. Still relying on his unlimited energy and his hot hand, Westbrook made 7 of his 17 three-point attempts and 12 of his

23 field goals to score a team-high 31 points. And despite the fact that he was arguably one of the smaller guys in the team, he led the West in rebounding as he grabbed eight boards en route to a 196-173 win and a consecutive All-Star Game MVP award. Russ became only the second player in league history to win the award back-to-back.

For a second straight year, Russell Westbrook channeled his inner Black Mamba to become the brightest of stars on the night when the biggest NBA superstar of the last 20 years was playing his final All-Star Game. Often regarded as Kobe Bryant's favorite player among the younger generation, Westbrook gave a lasting performance alongside the man he has likewise considered as one of his basketball idols growing up in Long Beach near Los Angeles. If he had a tribute to the retiring Kobe Bryant, it was that memorable performance in Toronto.

In his first game back after the All-Star break, Russell Westbrook would have 23 points and a new career high of 18 assists in a close loss to the Indiana Pacers and Paul George, who scored a game-high 41 points in the midseason classic barely a week before. Westbrook would then break the 40-point barrier for the fourth time that season by scoring 44 points on the New Orleans Pelicans on February 25. But despite the fact that Russ had been putting up insane numbers since the All-Star break, the Thunder had only won one of their last five games.

Russell Westbrook would momentarily break the skid of the Thunder by recording his 9th triple-double of the season on February 29 versus the Sacramento Kings in a win. He had 29 points, 13 rebounds, and 15 assists in that game. Though the Thunder would lose two straight games after that win, Westbrook would record two more triple-doubles in the following outings to cancel out their losses and to increase his triple-double count to 11 in the season. In his 11th triple-double, he had 25 points, 11 rebounds, and a new career high of 19 assists against the Los Angeles Clippers and Chris Paul, who was widely regarded as the better point guard of the two.

With Russell Westbrook going back to his stat-stuffing mentality, the Oklahoma City Thunder suddenly found themselves back on the winning track and peaking at the right moment just when the playoffs were nearing. In the first of what was going to be an eight-game winning streak for OKC, Westbrook had 17 points, ten rebounds, and 16 assists in only 28 minutes of action in a blowout win against the Trailblazers. Four days later, he would start a streak of his own as he recorded three consecutive triple-doubles for the Thunder to pull his league-leading count to 15. He finished the eight-game winning streak by posting 26 points, ten rebounds, and 12 assists. Westbrook would have two more triple-doubles for the season to end his campaign as the new Mr. Triple-Double with 18 of those for the year.

For the 2015-16 season, Russell Westbrook averaged some one of the greatest all-around numbers in recent years. He had 23.5 points, 7.8 rebounds, 10.4 assists, and 2.0 steals in 80 games of action and only 34 minutes per game. He led the league in triple-doubles as he garnered 18 of those that season to push his career total to 38. Before that season, he only had 20 triple-doubles in his career but quickly pushed himself to eighth all-time in that department.

While Russell Westbrook's impressive amount of triple-doubles were what made him a superstar and an All-NBA Team member that season, it was the improvement in his mentality as a leader and capacity to do everything on the floor at a high yet more efficient level that gave him the needed push to break through his personal barriers.

Though it was widely thought that Russell Westbrook had seen his peak during the 2014-15 season when Kevin Durant was out for most of the year, it was during the previously concluded season when Russ had reached the level of greatness not often seen, even in the long history of the NBA. His growth from his rookie year all the way to his eighth season in the NBA can never be measured by numbers as statistics alone could not give justice to how good Westbrook has been over the last 82-game stretch.

The first noticeable improvement to Westbrook's game was how well he had grown as a passer. At the start of his career in the league, he never had the same vision, IQ, or mentality that playmakers like Kidd, Nash, and Paul always had. He was looking to attack more often that he passed the ball. But Russ suddenly became a different player during the 2015-16 season when he was opting to set his teammates up more instead of looking for shots. Westbrook learned how to slow the game down so that he could keep his passing skills on par with his ability to go as fast as he could.[xiv] And with the tutelage and the new ball-sharing style that Billy Donovan implemented, Russ seemed like a combination of Jason Kidd and Chris Paul out there.

Westbrook also learned how to channel his athleticism and his natural nose for the ball even further by ganging up for rebounds and hustling for loose balls and possessions. Always regarded as a great rebounding point guard, Westbrook upped the ante by nearly pulling down eight boards per game for a guy barely standing 6'3". But his rebounding numbers were not a function of the Thunder's lack of rebounders. Russ was playing alongside four other good rebounders in Enes Kanter, Steven Adams, Serge Ibaka, and Kevin Durant, but still made it a point to gang up on rebounds to suddenly push the ball up for quick transition plays. The Thunder, thanks in large part to Westbrook's willingness to rebound, were by far the best rebounding team in the NBA that season.

Best of all, despite the fact that he had just come off a season wherein he was the best scorer in the league, he never tried to take over games by himself. Instead, he was playing within the flow of the game and even attempted fewer shots that season as Kevin Durant was coming back to the form that had helped him win the MVP in 2014. Westbrook had learned to be mature and efficient with his shot selection, but was still able to put up incredible offensive numbers if he needed to.

Long regarded as a selfish player that only cared about putting up good statistics while shooting inefficient attempts he deprived away from Kevin Durant, Westbrook became one of the most valuable players in the NBA in his 8th season in the league. It was not because he changed his style, but because he used the same ferocity, intensity, and emotion to fuel himself to reach another level. Russell Westbrook, as Kevin Durant said himself two seasons ago, never had to change himself to make people realize his worth and value. Westbrook's beastly qualities would only serve the OKC Thunder better in what was to become another deep playoff run for them. As Billy Donovan would put it, he let Russell Westbrook be himself instead of being a passing playmaker or an attacking point guard.[xiv]

The playoff run for the Thunder began against the Dallas Mavericks, who they quickly dispatched in five games. In a 38-point Game 1 victory, Russell Westbrook was at his most efficient when he had 24 points and 11 assists in barely 30 minutes of action. He would have 19 points and 14 rebounds in Game 2 when the Mavericks won their only game.

Russell Westbrook was not someone to be trifled with after losing Game 2 at home. In Game 3 in Dallas, he had 26 points and 15 assists while not even trying to rebound at least one board for a 29-point win. Still playing the role of a passer, he had 25 points and 15 assists in Game 4 to lead his team to a 3-1 lead before finishing things off with a near triple-double effort in Game 5. In that closeout game, he had 36 points, 12 rebounds, and nine assists while averaging 26 points, 7.2 rebounds, and 11.2 assists in that five-game series.

After beating the Dallas Mavericks in a relatively easy series in the first round, the Oklahoma City Thunder were suddenly humbled by the 67-win San Antonio Spurs in Game 1 of their second-round matchup. In that 32-point loss to the Spurs, Russ only had 14 points and nine assists in an embarrassing effort for the team. OKC, however, would exact revenge in Game 2, which featured a controversial ending that resulted in a win for the Thunder. Westbrook had 29 points, seven rebounds, and ten assists in that game.

While nearly putting up a triple-double effort and shooting inefficiently from the field in Game 3, Russell Westbrook could not muster up enough energy to lead his team to victory in that four-point loss. But despite shooting another dismal clip from the floor, it was his playmaking that got the Thunder a win in Game 4 to tie the series 2-2. He had 14 points, seven rebounds, and 15 assists in that match.

In yet another controversial finish, the OKC Thunder would take the series lead for good after beating the San Antonio Spurs in Game 5 of their Western Conference Semifinals matchup. Russ had 35 points, 11 rebounds, and nine assists in another near triple-double effort for the league's leader in that department. And banking on the energy from their home crowd while peaking at the best moment to possibly win a title, the Thunder won Game 6 to close the series out and reach the Western Conference Finals. Westbrook had 28 points and 12 assists in that game.

Though Russell Westbrook and the OKC Thunder were about to face the historic 73-win Golden State Warriors in the Conference Finals, they were still regarded as favorites to win the series because they were peaking at the right time and they had all the confidence in the world after upsetting the San Antonio Spurs. More importantly, the Thunder were the bigger, hungrier, and more athletic team in that matchup. They had all the tools to beat the Warriors and get to the NBA Finals for the first time since 2012.

Matched up against the smaller and less athletic Stephen Curry, who had just been named as the first ever unanimous MVP in league history, Westbrook took the match up personally as he physically abused Curry's defense to the point that the Warriors had to switch Klay Thompson on him. It did not matter. Russ finished the game with 27 points, 12 assists, and seven steals to draw first blood in the series.

Though the Warriors managed to exact revenge by winning Game 2 by 27 points, the Thunder and their fiery superstar point guard were in full effect in Games 3 and 4. In the third game of the series, Russ abused the Warrior defense again to go for 30 points, eight rebounds, and 12 assists in that 28-point win. Winning the game by 24 points, the Thunder relied on

Westbrook's triple-double of 36 points, 11 rebounds, and 11 assists to take Game 4 away and to lead the series 3-1.

With only one win separating them from a possible trip to the NBA Finals, the Oklahoma City Thunder were in the best position to finally win a title for the franchise and for their two superstars, who were both hungry for rings. But there was a reason why the Golden State Warriors were the defending champions and why they had won 73 games in the regular season. They came back with a strong flurry.

Thanks to the resurgent play of the two-time MVP, the Warriors were able to take Game 5 away to live at least another day against the Thunder, who both saw spectacular scoring efforts from both Durant and Westbrook in that game. In Game 6, the Thunder were already smelling the Finals, especially since they were leading well entering the fourth quarter. But the phenomenal outside sniping of Klay Thompson and Steph Curry suddenly put the game back in the hands of the Warriors, who pushed the series to seven games.

Russell Westbrook and his team suddenly found themselves in an uncomfortable situation. A few games ago, they were leading 3-1 and just needed a win to go the Finals. But the Warriors all but erased the lead and forced a deciding Game 7 in the Bay

Area. Wanting to avoid a monumental meltdown, the Thunder would rely on their dynamic duo yet again.

Unfortunately for Russ, he was shooting blanks all game long and could not match the outside sniping and energy that the Warriors backcourt had. He was limited to 19 points, though he had 13 assists in a tough shooting night for him and Durant. Meanwhile on the other end, Steph and Klay were both connecting on their shots to help the Warriors win Game 7 after facing a 1-3 deficit. The meltdown was complete, and the Thunder had to go home suffering three straight losses that could have gone their way.

After the 3-1 meltdown that the Thunder faced in the Western Conference Finals, questions arose about the team's future. There were no more doubts of whether Kevin Durant and Russell Westbrook could coexist and form a championship-contending duo. The two superstars had already shown enough chemistry, familiarity, and adoration for one another in their eight years together as the league's best duo. But the question was whether they were going to stay a pair for at least one more season.

Having dominated the league with their combination of size, length, and athleticism, KD and Russ were arguably the best duo of their generation. They were the Shaq and Kobe of the recent era. But unlike the Diesel and the Mamba, they were not able to win a title as a duo. They did make the Finals in 2012 only to lose to the hunger and experience of the Heat. Their best chance was recently thrown away after losing a 3-1 lead to the Warriors. Despite what we are told to believe in, neither Durant nor Russ was to blame for that meltdown in 2016. There was a reason why the Warriors were champions and why they won 73 games in one season. They showed that when they came back to win the series.

Having blown away their chance to win a title, it was doubtful whether they could mount another similar monumental run, particularly since the rest of the Western Conference was improving and rising to the challenge of the Warriors and the Spurs. On another note, the Thunder were also facing the problem of keeping their core duo intact. Kevin Durant was a free agent in the offseason while Russell Westbrook was going to be one after a year.

On his part, Kevin Durant went out to entertain offers from several teams that had huge salary cap spaces. Unfortunately for the Thunder, several of those teams were already contenders. If not, they were either improving to be contenders or were storied franchises in the NBA. When the Washington Wizards, Boston Celtics, and Los Angeles Lakers among others tried their hand at wooing Durant away from the Thunder, the Spurs and the Warriors were the best contenders for the services of the 2014 NBA MVP. However, at the end of it all, KD decided to go to the Bay Area to join the already dominant team of the Golden State Warriors.

In their quest to convince Kevin Durant to stay in Oklahoma, the Thunder actually made several roster changes. They first traded away their third best player Serge Ibaka over to the Orlando Magic to get young and rising athletic guard Victor Oladipo and outside specialist big man Ersan Ilyasova. They also would not retain the services of Dion Waiters, who went to the Miami Heat in the offseason.

With Kevin Durant already gone, the question was now whether Russell Westbrook would use the same card that KD played and go to another team. As Russ was unsure of staying in OKC, the Thunder entertained several trade talks involving the superstar point guard. Durant's sudden decision made the Thunder a shell of their former selves and also got Westbrook rethinking about the team's future now that their best player was gone.[xv] He had a choice of whether to force himself for a trade that offseason, or to play it out at least one more season in Oklahoma City and join the free agency fever in 2017.

"Loyalty is something I stand by." Those were the word uttered by Russell Westbrook when he finally decided to stay with the Thunder after signing a three-year $86 million contract extension with the team despite the unsure future that OKC has with the major roster changes they implemented. Westbrook, the man often criticized for his selfishness, was the loyal one that chose to stay with the team that trusted him and drafted him for eight whole seasons.

With the decision to remain in OKC all but behind him, Russell Westbrook was going to enter a 2016-17 season that might see him exploding out of the scene for one of the best statistical seasons the league might ever see. We have already seen what Russ could do as a lone superstar when Durant was injured in 2015. We have also seen what he could do as an all-around beast when the Thunder were peaking at the right time in 2016. But with the world anticipating that Westbrook would put on a one-man show for the Thunder in the upcoming season, talks suddenly surfaced about the point guard's possible MVP run because of the monstrous numbers he was predicted to put up.

ESPN projects Russell Westbrook to finish second to only Steph Curry in the MVP race in the 2016-17 season due to his penchant to put up all-around monstrous numbers on every facet of the game.[xvi] He is even a favorite to win the league's scoring title once again considering that Curry and Durant, two of the league's best scorers, are playing together in one team. With that said and done, it is almost an assurance that Russell Westbrook will become Beastbrook again in the upcoming 2016-17 season. All the world has to do is to brace themselves and watch out for the show that Russ will put on once the season gets started.

Chapter 5: Westbrook's Personal Life

The NBA had an image problem in 2005. The league was reeling from the sexual assault charges against Kobe Bryant, the 2004 Pacers-Pistons brawl which had spilled into the stands, and a 2005 NBA Finals that received record-low ratings and was described as a boring and ugly battle between two defensive teams in San Antonio and Detroit. Many fans were also concerned about the growing connections between the NBA and the hip-hop world. To address these concerns, in 2005, the NBA decided to implement a dress code. Players attending the games who were not in uniform due to injury were required to wear a sport coat and dress shoes, while NBA players, in general, had to wear "business casual" attire. Sunglasses while indoors, chains, t-shirts, and other casual wear were banned.

Many initially protested the ban, declaring that it was an attack against hip-hop culture and would not change a thing. Allen Iverson stated that "a murderer in a suit is still a murderer," and even the placid, calm Tim Duncan called the dress code "a load of crap." Despite these complaints, NBA players adhered to the NBA's regulations and wore standard black and blue sports coats or suits when they sat on the bench or appeared in post-game press conferences. As occurs so often when an authority figure issues a new controversial regulation, NBA players have adapted over the years to stay within the bounds of "business casual" while still showing their sense of style.

Russell Westbrook is right there leading the charge of fashionable formality. During standard post-game press conferences, Westbrook consistently wore highly colorful and vibrant Polos and dress shirts. At one time, he even wore a shirt that was emblazoned with giant pictures of M&Ms. Westbrook also wears colorful, thick-rimmed glasses similar to those of a stereotypical nerd, a unique contrast for one of the best athletes in the United States. Westbrook's fashion is just as outlandish outside the press conferences. He has been spotted wearing leopard prints, a shirt filled with pictures of fishing lures, suspenders with a bowtie, and other ridiculous styles. For most people, such clothing choices would be a ludicrous fashion *faux pas*. Westbrook, however, was always able to wear such things with confidence. He declares that he has always loved fashion, and in November 2013, he signed an endorsement deal with Kings and Jax Boxer Briefs.

Perhaps no accessory carries more weight for Westbrook than the wristband he wears on his right arm bearing "KB3," a lasting tribute to Khelcey Barrs III, a childhood friend and teammate who died in 2004 from an enlarged heart during a pickup game. After the untimely passing of his friend,

Westbrook made it a point to stop by Barrs' grandmother's house to take the trash out for the week, just like how his departed friend did for many years. In many ways, it seems like fate stepped in for Westbrook. You see, before Barrs' passing, he was actively recruited by UCLA.

Fashion is not the only thing that preoccupies Westbrook. A young Westbrook began learning basketball out of the desire to earn a college scholarship. Although Westbrook left college after his sophomore year to enter the NBA, he went back to UCLA during the summer to finish his degree. He finally graduated in 2011.

Family is also one of the most important things for Westbrook. He often gives a lot of praise to his family during interviews. He has still not forgotten about the many times he and his father shot jumpers inside the gym. Rather than spending his time around nightclubs where nothing good ever happens, he prefers to spend time with his little brother during trips back home.

Talents aside, Westbrook has become not only a cornerstone of the Thunder's franchise but also a face to the community of Oklahoma City. Humility and fame are two words seldom seen together. Nevertheless, Westbrook's humility is an embodiment of all of the hard work and sacrifice he made to get to the top. As such, he is heavily involved in the community.

In 2012, he launched his Why Not? Foundation. To get his foundation off to a big start, he hosted two Thanksgiving Dinners. While Westbrook spent Thanksgiving providing dinner to needy families in Oklahoma, his parents and brother served over four hundred disadvantaged people in the very same recreation park he learned how to play basketball in. Stories like this are common throughout the community. Additionally, each Christmas, Westbrook provides disadvantaged children with backpacks filled with presents as well as Jordan sneakers. As Westbrook explains, giving back to the community that supports him is what defines the holidays.

"More and more children are placed into foster care each year, and to be in a position to bring the joy of Christmas to some of these kids is truly a blessing," he said. "I am in a unique position to be able to give back to a community that has been so supportive of me, and help children in need." In 2014, his generosity extended into the classroom through the Russell Reading Room Initiative. Its goal is to increase literacy among children in the area by providing students access to books throughout schools in Oklahoma.

When Westbrook was named the 2015 NBA All-Star Game MVP last February, he received a brand new SUV from Kia as part of the car maker's sponsorship of the NBA's Mid-Season

Classic. While that kind of motor vehicle may not be moving for a highly-paid NBA superstar like him, what Westbrook did with it was.

Through his Why Not? Foundation, Westbrook decided to dish off a different kind of assist outside of the basketball court and gave the car to someone who needed it more than he did. The foundation sought the assistance of Sunbeam Family Services, a local organization that provided social programs and services for low-income Oklahomans, to search for a deserving beneficiary. The agency selected 19-year-old single mother Kerstin Gonzalez, a graduating high school student who was hoping to continue higher education while raising her two children. Gonzalez had been borrowing cars from her family and friends so that she could manage her time well and keep up with her busy schedule of going to school, getting to work, and picking up her two boys. Gonzalez was moved to tears when she learned of Westbrook's donation. Westbrook did not stop there. He also committed to pay for the first year of insurance, registration, and other fees related to putting the SUV on the road.

Westbrook's act of giving may have looked nothing extraordinary because the car did not mean much to him. However, for Kerstin, it was the world, and that is the essence here. That was what mattered. Westbrook gave something tangible to someone he never met before, someone who needed the car more than he did. It showed a compassionate side of a furious basketball competitor.

Chapter 6: Impact on Basketball

Over the course of his NBA career, Westbrook has had the good fortune of blossoming in an age when the point guard is more valuable than ever before. In the past, it was the big man who dominated the NBA. Most of the all-time greats in NBA history, such as Bill Russell, Kareem Abdul-Jabbar, Hakeem Olajuwon, or Shaquille O'Neal, were all big men. While Michael Jordan was obviously no big man, part of what made him so incredible was the fact that he was able to dominate the league so thoroughly, winning title after title, even though he never played like a truly great big man. Dennis Rodman was an excellent rebounder. He was 34 when he joined the Bulls and never made the All-Star Team as a Bull. The logic for so long has been that a team with the best big man combination will be the team that triumphs in the playoffs, barring spectacular talents like LeBron James or Michael Jordan.

However, things have begun to change in the NBA. There is more importance placed on the 3-point shot compared to the past. Changes in defensive rules have made doubling a big man in the post easier than before. Due to these changes, there has been less of an importance on post play. Furthermore, there has been an influx of new, athletic score-first point guards, who seek to score for themselves as much as they pass and set up the offense. Such point guards are nothing new – the 2000s had Allen Iverson, Steve Francis, Allan Houston, and Stephon Marbury, among others, and before them, there were Jerry West and Isiah Thomas. But there has never been as many scoring point guards as there are today. As the 2015 season showed us, practically every single one of the top Western Conference teams has a dynamic scoring point guard such as Russell Westbrook, Chris Paul, Stephen Curry, or Damian Lillard.

While players like Curry or Lillard depend a great deal on the 3-point shot to score, Westbrook is different. He has never been a great 3-point shooter, averaging 30% for his career and never more than 33% in a season. Instead, Westbrook relies on his blinding athleticism and terrific passing skills. His 3-point shot may be unreliable, but Westbrook's mid-range game is excellent. The Thunder has excellent screeners in Nick Collison and Serge Ibaka, and all it takes is one good screen for Westbrook to get open in the lane. Once open, he will take the mid-range shot, drive to the lane, or pass it off to Durant or another cutting roll man. There are point guards who are better passers than Westbrook, but Westbrook's combination of athleticism and passing ability is entirely unique. This makes him one of the most dangerous offensive threats in the league today. None of that even begins to touch on his devastating transition game, where Westbrook can outrun nearly anyone for a thunderous slam-dunk. And when he wants to attack the basket, he is nigh impossible to stop and always makes it a point to finish strong and ferociously.

However, even with the rule changes and the rise of great point guards like Westbrook, concerns remain about how truly essential the point guard is, especially in comparison to the tried and true method of inside domination and post play. The Miami Heat, in their championship years, did not have an elite point guard, and neither did the Dallas Mavericks before them nor did the Los Angeles Lakers. Only the Spurs and the Warriors have had All-Star level point guards in their championship seasons.

In the cases of the Heat, Lakers, and Mavs, a primary reason for their championships was the ability to score in the post, whether it was Pau Gasol, Dirk Nowitzki, or LeBron. The San Antonio Spurs, the pinnacle of basketball excellence, have one of the best scoring point guards in Tony Parker, but they also have Tim Duncan, who remains one of the best post players today. A point guard like Westbrook may score points and notch assists, but the Thunder has absolutely no reliable players down in the post. They rely heavily on jump shots and the ability of Westbrook and Durant to drive inside. Can such a new style of play which is dependent on Westbrook's athletic and intelligent play win a title?

Another question which arises with the rise of athletic scoring point guards is their longevity, an issue that is particularly relevant for Westbrook, given his recent injury history. The athletic scoring point guards of the past flamed out spectacularly. Steve Francis went from being a starting point guard in the 2004 All-Star Game to being washed up by 2006. Allen Iverson was a key piece on the Denver Nuggets team that won 50 games in 2008 but was out of the league by 2010. Derrick Rose won the MVP in 2011, but now, after battling one knee injury after another, there are serious concerns about whether he will be an All-Star again. Can Westbrook avoid the fate that point guards similar to him have experienced when he grows older? He is in his peak form right now, and so far, he has rebounded well enough despite struggling with injuries recently. While there may be more point guards who seek to score for themselves than ever before, it is Westbrook, with his combination of athleticism and passing ability, who will represent whether they can be a vital part of a championship team, or if they are just a fad that will fade over time.

Chapter 7: Russell Westbrook's Legacy and Future

Russell Westbrook will go down in NBA history as probably the most athletic point guard in the history of the NBA. While there have been a lot of fast and high-flying point guards in the NBA, none of them have had the combination of Westbrook's skillset, speed, and leaping ability. Westbrook is so blindingly fast that he can outrun any player in the NBA. The only player today that could rival his speed is John Wall of the Washington Wizards. When attacking the basket or grabbing rebounds, one can see how high Westbrook leaps. He is truly an athletic freak of nature. We know how good of an athlete he is, but his skillset is not too shabby, either. Russ evolved from an attacking shooting guard in college to one of the best point guards in today's NBA. His offensive game is complete, and he can shoot from anywhere on the floor, create open shots off the dribble, and attack the basket with reckless abandon. As a passer, he has also evolved into a true point guard, quickly involving his teammates in the flow of the offense.

While there have been players that have the same skillset and athletic abilities of a Russell Westbrook, none of them were the type of player he is. Derrick Rose, in his early years, was just as athletic and skillful as today's Westbrook. But he could not stay healthy, and just did not have the same drive that Russ has. John Wall can get off the floor high and may even be faster than Westbrook, but he does not have the attacking mentality or the motor of Russ. What sets Russell Westbrook apart from those types of players is his ferocity, intensity, and his drive on doing whatever he can on the floor.

Russ always makes it a point to put every ounce of his energy into every play on the basketball court. He puts the same amount of intensity he does on the defensive end as he does on offense. While that power and ferocity made him out of control early in his career, he has since learned how to channel and control it. While Westbrook has a good demeanor, he is arguably the angriest man in the league whenever he attacks the basket. He plays with such ferocity that NBA TV analyst Shaquille O'Neal calls him "Little Rage" because of the seemingly angry way he plays the game despite his size. Even Kobe Bryant in "Kobe: The Interview," said that Russell Westbrook is the meanest NBA player on the court and is his favorite player today because he reminded him so much of himself. Russ was just as competitive and as ferocious of a player as Kobe was in his early days.[xvii]

With that, Westbrook will somehow end his career as one of the best point guards in the NBA and may even be one of the best players in history if he can stay healthy and play at a high level throughout his career, or if he can win several championships along the way.

For the OKC Thunder, Russell Westbrook is the best point guard in franchise history, ever since the franchise relocated to Oklahoma City. Remembering back to their days in Seattle, the franchise has had the luxury of point guard Gary Payton playing for them. Payton may be the best point guard in the Sonics/Thunder franchise history, but Russell Westbrook is quickly creeping up to him and may even be as good as Payton was in his prime. Barring injuries or any other setbacks, Westbrook will become the best point guard in Sonics/Thunder history as long as he stays with the team for several more years. Overall, Russell Westbrook also has a chance of becoming the best player in franchise history. Some may argue that Kevin Durant is already the best player in Sonics/Thunder franchise history because of his transcendent scoring that won him the MVP award. However, now that Kevin Durant has chosen to chase titles in another pasture, Russell Westbrook has what it takes to solidify himself as the Thunder's best player and one of the most prolific players of his generation.

The Western Conference is never an easy battle, and the Thunder will need Westbrook to play his usual self to secure their first title. Westbrook, who has been so continually doubted throughout his career, is used to pressure. He went from a player who failed to make his high school varsity team until his junior year to a college bench player, and eventually, to the number 4 pick in the 2008 NBA Draft. There were doubts about whether or not he should have been picked that high, but Westbrook's hard work and dedication to basketball helped him steadily develop into one of the premier point guards in the NBA. Even at that pinnacle, a few doubts remain about his play. Is he too selfish and too concerned with looking out for his numbers? Can a point guard be one the primary option for a championship team in what has traditionally been a league dominated by big men, especially now that Durant has gone elsewhere? These doubts were seemingly quelled after Oklahoma City showed to be a weaker team without Westbrook. But with Oklahoma City still winning 59 games in the 2013-2014 season, and despite Westbrook missing over half of the season, criticisms started up again, only to be silenced by Russ's phenomenal seasons in 2014-15 and 2015-16. No matter what happens, the doubts will likely never disappear until the Thunder wins the NBA Finals. Nevertheless, even if he never wins the NBA title, rest assured that there will probably never be another point guard that plays the game of basketball the same way as Russell Westbrook has throughout his career.

Final Word/About the Author

I was born and raised in Norwalk, Connecticut. Growing up, I could often be found spending many nights watching basketball, soccer, and football matches with my father in the family living room. I love sports and everything that sports can embody. I believe that sports are one of most genuine forms of competition, heart, and determination. I write my works to learn more about influential athletes in the hopes that from my writing, you the reader can walk away inspired to put in an equal if not greater amount of hard work and perseverance to pursue your goals. If you enjoyed *Russell Westbrook: The Inspiring Story of One of Basketball's Premier Point Guards,* please leave a review! Also, you can read more of my works on *Brett Favre, Calvin Johnson, Drew Brees, J.J. Watt, Colin Kaepernick, Aaron Rodgers, Peyton Manning, Tom Brady, Russell Wilson, Michael Jordan, LeBron James, Kyrie Irving, Klay Thompson, Stephen Curry, Kevin Durant, Russell Westbrook, Anthony Davis, Chris Paul, Blake Griffin, Kobe Bryant, Joakim Noah, Scottie Pippen, Carmelo Anthony, Kevin Love, Grant Hill, Tracy McGrady, Vince Carter, Patrick Ewing, Karl Malone, Tony Parker, Allen Iverson, Hakeem Olajuwon, Reggie Miller, Michael Carter-Williams, John Wall, James Harden, Tim Duncan, Steve Nash, Draymond Green, Kawhi Leonard, Dwyane Wade, Ray Allen,*

Pau Gasol, Dirk Nowitzki, Jimmy Butler, Paul Pierce, Manu Ginobili, Pete Maravich, Larry Bird, Kyle Lowry, Jason Kidd, David Robinson, LaMarcus Aldridge, Derrick Rose, Paul George, Kevin Garnett, Chris Paul and Marc Gasol in the Kindle Store. If you love basketball, check out my website at claytongeoffreys.com to join my exclusive list where I let you know about my latest books and give you lots of goodies.

Like what you read? Please leave a review!

I write because I love sharing the stories of influential people like Russell Westbrook with fantastic readers like you. My readers inspire me to write more so please do not hesitate to let me know what you thought by leaving a review! If you love books on life, basketball, or productivity, check out my website at claytongeoffreys.com to join my exclusive list where I let you know about my latest books. Aside from being the first to hear about my latest releases, you can also download a free copy of *33 Life Lessons: Success Principles, Career Advice & Habits of Successful People*. See you there!

Clayton

References

[i] Russell Westbrook". *Biography*. Web.

[ii] Mayberry, Darnel. ""Russell Westbrook's journey from community center gyms to the NBA All-Star game". *News OK.* 19 February 2011. Web.

[iii] Mayberry, Darnel. "Russell Westbrook's journey from community center gyms to the NBA All-Star game". *News OK.* 19 February 2011. Web.

[iv] "Russell Westbrook". *NBA Draft*. Web.

[v] "Russell Westbrook". *DraftExpress*. Web.

[vi] "Russell Westbrook". *DraftExpress*. Web.

[vii] "Russell Westbrook". *DraftExpress*. Web.

[viii] "Russell Westbrook". *DraftExpress*. Web.

[ix] "Russell Westbrook". *DraftExpress*. Web.

[x] Young, Royce. "Russell Westbrook's Jumper, Then and Now". *Daily Thunder*. 1 June 2011. Web

[xi] Mahoney, Rob. "Is Russell Westbrook the Most Unfairly Criticized Star in the NBA?". *Bleacher Report*. 28 September 2012. Web

[xii] Favale, Dan. "Is the Constant Critique of Russell Westbrook's Game Fair or Foul?". *Bleacher Report.* 29 January 2013. Web

[xiii] Horne, Erik. "OKC Thunder: Is There Room for Even More Improvement in Russell Westbrook's Game?". *The Oklahoman*. 3 October 2015. Web

[xiv] Young, Royce. "The Evolution of Russell Westbrook is Complete". *ESPN*. 18 November 2015. Web

[xv] Young, Royce. "Kevin Durant's Defection Forcing Westbrook to Decide OKC Future Now". *ESPN*. 27 July 2016. Web

[xvi] Horne, Erik. "Russell Westbrook Ranks Second in MVP Projections by ESPN". *The Oklahoman*. 28 July 2016. Web

[xvii] Hansford, Corey. "Kobe Bryant on Russell Westbrook: 'He Plays Mean Like I Did'". *Lakers Nation*. 17 February 2015. Web.

Made in the USA
San Bernardino, CA
19 April 2017